Frederick Law Olmsted's New York

Text by Elizabeth Barlow

Illustrative Portfolio by William Alex

Praeger Publishers

New York • Washington • London

In association with the Whitney Museum of American Art

Frederick Law Olmsted's New York was initially published on the occasion of an exhibition of the same title presented by the Whitney Museum of American Art in New York City from October 19 through December 3, 1972, organized and directed by William Alex and supported by grants from The J. M. Kaplan Fund and the Graham Foundation for Advanced Studies in the Fine Arts.

PRAEGER PUBLISHERS
111 Fourth Avenue, New York, N.Y. 10003, U.S.A.
5, Cromwell Place, London SW7 2JL, England

Published in the United States of America in 1972
by Praeger Publishers, Inc.,
in association with the Whitney Museum of American Art
© 1972 by the Whitney Museum of American Art

Library of Congress Catalog Card Number: 72–82771

Designed by Joseph Bourke Del Valle

Printed in the United States of America

Contents

Introduction

At the time of his birth a career such as the one for which Frederick Law Olmsted eventually became famous was almost beyond imagining. When America's first landscape architect and city planner was born in Hartford, Connecticut, on April 26, 1822, open countryside was easily accessible to town dwellers, and rural sounds and odors permeated urban life. Hogs were the sanitationmen of the day, collecting garbage from gutters, and steaming manure smells rather than carbon monoxide filled the air. To introduce nature within the urban sphere would have seemed irrelevant, unnecessary.

True, for pragmatic reasons, central-city open space was indeed reserved: the village green for common pasturage, the parade ground for military drill, the residential square to set neighborhood tone. It was true, too, that Americans were beginning to adopt a new attitude toward nature. Following distinctions that had been enunciated in England at the end of the eighteenth century, writers and travelers about this time began classifying landscapes into aesthetic categories. The wilderness cult gradually permeated religion and philosophy, and the stern Calvinist God of the Scriptures was gradually replaced by the concept of God in Nature, as Americans sought examples of His hand in the forests and on the mountaintops.

Few people in 1822, however, looked for anything good or beautiful in the cities. Thomas Jefferson had firmly declared them pernicious to the moral health of the nation, although in 1816 he was forced to admit "that to be independent for the comforts of life . . . we must now place the manufacturer by the side of the agriculturist." In other words, America should have cities grudgingly, out of necessity, but her self-image should be agrarian, pastoral.

Olmsted's birth roughly coincided with the birth of technology in America, and it would be impossible to ignore for long the immense stimulus technology exerted upon urbanization and the fact that there really was no turning back to Jefferson's original arcadian vision of a completely pastoral America. Fifteen years before Olmsted was born, Robert Fulton had successfully demonstrated the miracle of steam power for water transport; when Olmsted was three, the growth of commercial towns in upstate New York was made possible by the opening of the Erie Canal; and when he was eight the laying of the first rails of the Baltimore and Ohio line allowed a new breed of utopians to begin dreaming of a network of cities stretching across the all-but-untenanted continent.

Jefferson, a child of the Enlightenment, was enthusiastic about the new labor-saving inventions of the age, and Americans in general felt a great sense of pleasurable awe as the wonders of industrial technology became manifest. Few people sensed there was anything incompatible between Progress and Nature. Certainly no one worried very much over the *design* of the rapidly mushrooming new cities or the expanding old ones and the consequences of their planning, or lack of planning, upon the lives of their inhabitants. Nature could be innocently eradicated wherever necessary to accommodate urban growth. For a while at least, it seemed possible that America could have both its factories and its pure and sparkling streams; somehow, in the New World, technology would not betray the promise of the good life by creating ugly and socially harmful environments as it had in the Old.

Commercial growth and industrial wealth fed another impulse that gathered momentum in the decade preceding the Civil War. As the concerns of the country became increasingly materialistic, Americans focused less on the spiritual woes and the Dickensian misery of the bad, old European cities and more on the features that made them entertaining, cultured, and civilized. The post-Revolutionary chauvinism that put a premium, as Jefferson had done, on rustic simplicity and native innocence began to wear thin, and a desire to emulate European elegance and sophistication with a variety of civic embellishments grew. In short, Americans had begun to feel self-consciously provincial, and, while untutored primitivism remained a heroic myth for the frontier, upper-class city dwellers desired concert halls, libraries, museums—and parks.

Paradoxically, a growing awareness of the social cost of industrialism (and it was, of course, newly generated industrial wealth that made possible the creation of these urban jewels in the first place) stimulated a widespread sentimental reverence for nature as a spiritual balm and antidote to the increasingly frenetic, dehumanizing aspects of city life. Elegiac, landscaped cemeteries such as Mount Auburn in Boston and Greenwood in Brooklyn replaced churchyards as burial grounds, and they became favorite Sunday visiting spots in the 1840's. They must have helped stimulate the desire for pleasure grounds without pathos, particularly as American travelers returned from abroad impressed by the municipal parks they had seen.

Cities continued to grow at an ever accelerating rate, but no longer in a random way, as they had before the nineteenth century. Their form was in most cases dictated by the rigid rules of geometry. New York had since 1811 been marching steadily uptown to the uniform beat of its official gridiron plan. No deviation to accommodate natural topography was thought necessary. The regularity of rectangular blocks and standard-size lots simplified the task of the surveyor and the profit calculations of the real estate speculator.

Between the time of Olmsted's birth and the time he took up residence in New York some thirty years later, the city's population had more than tripled its growth, from 125,000 to 425,000. While the old Brownstone New York of the 1850's would probably appear quaintly charming to our automobile-assaulted twentieth-century eyes, people then complained loudly of its dirt, noise, and ugliness and of its festering urban pathologies—crowded and unhygienic slums, official corruption, gang warfare.

Greenwood Cemetery, 1867.

The cases for and against urbanization had obviously grown much thornier and complex than they had been in Jefferson's day.

Olmsted felt conflicting emotions toward the city, and out of his ambivalence arose his great contributions to it. He was primarily a Jeffersonian at heart, but at the same time he put a high premium on the value of "civilization" and its accompanying social and material amenities. As a young man, he turned his hand to farming, enthusiastically applying the latest principles of agricultural science to a fruit-tree nursery on Staten Island. Even when he abandoned this line of work to become a traveling journalist, first in England and then in the South, he maintained a Jeffersonian self-image, signing his literary productions "Yeoman" and "An American Farmer."

Though he read the transcendentalists with admiration, he was too objective, too "gentlemanly" perhaps, to subscribe to their radicalism. It is his aristocratic paternalism, as well as his somewhat wooden prose style, that makes him so much less accessible as a person to us today than Thoreau. Thoreau's simplicity and desire to abandon the materialism of civilized society put him, unlike Olmsted, in tune with contemporary existentialism and despairing anti-urbanism. Still, Olmsted did what Thoreau could not have done and would not have cared to do: he did not turn his back on the process of American urbanization; rather, he took the Jeffersonian rural ideal and carried it into the heart of the city. It is for putting a great and wonderful village green— a village green enlarged to a metropolitan scale—in the middle of New York City that Olmsted is chiefly remembered, not that Central Park is his best work but because it is, as Henry James remarked, "the cheerful, capable, bustling, even if overworked, hostess of the one inn, somewhere, who has to take all the travel."

Like the Beaux Arts architects, he tried to stamp the city with an ennobling vision. Olmsted's parks were designed to be elegant, elevating, educational. But, whereas Richard Morris Hunt and Stanford White turned out buildings of eclectic grandeur, Olmsted's sympathies were more attuned to the style of H. H. Richardson, his friend and frequent collaborator. His sources of inspiration did not lie in Greece, Rome, or France, but rather in England.

He was more than an arranger of bucolic scenes, however. He was the country's first transportation planner, introducing in the Central Park transverse roads the principle of grade separation of traffic. As he matured in his profession, he came to regard landscapes as kinetic, sequential experiences in which memory and anticipation played important roles. Both the word "parkway" and its concept are his.

Olmsted extended his practice of designing with nature from the scale of the individual park to that of the city-wide park system. Utilizing natural drainage patterns, he wove chains of green through the gray warp and woof of the urban grid, stringing together like emeralds on a necklace large parks, such as those that he designed in Buffalo and Boston. In his schemes for the development of northern Manhattan and for Staten Island, which unfortunately were never realized, and for Riverside, a suburb of Chicago that was built according to his plan, he laid out curvilinear streets following natural topographic features. By developing a hierarchy of roads, he established the idea of segregating residential and commercial traffic.

It was, of course, machine technology—specifically the technology of rail transportation—that made possible Olmsted's suburban solution as an alternative to life in the compacted central city. That suburban ideal, so innovative for its time, is now somewhat discredited. Less capable designers have turned curvilinear streets into a formula as sterile as the conventional grid, and the advent of the automobile has caused the line of demarcation between the city and the surrounding country to become increasingly blurred and distended by a blanket of look-alike houses.

The affluence of post-Civil War industrialization gave rise to the Gilded Age and brought Olmsted a new set of clients. Vanderbilts and Rockefellers engaged him to lay out the grounds of their estates. He was retained as campus planner of a long list of schools and colleges including Lawrenceville, Groton, Colgate, Amherst, Smith, and Stanford. Cities all across the country wanted their municipal parks laid out by the acknowledged master, and Olmsted found himself on trains traveling to Louisville, Kansas City, Milwaukee, and Rochester. In Washington, D.C., he designed the grounds of the Capitol, and proposed the present terrace and parapet on its West Side, a departure from the usual leitmotif of rural scenery that characterized most of his work.

Besides being a gifted artist, Olmsted was also a social reformer. He served as the executive secretary of the United States Sanitary Commission (the forerunner of the Red Cross) during the Civil War, and out of that experience grew his concern and expertise in the field of public health, which is reflected in his 1871 Report to the Staten Island Improvement Commission. He campaigned for Yosemite, the country's first national park and for the preservation of Niagara Falls from the cancerous growth of commercial honky-tonk that was eating away the scenery on its periphery.

Olmsted's style of planning and park design, his use of nature to humanize the city and soften its hard edges, was at last superseded by another approach, that of the City Beautiful, with its emphasis on public architecture of neoclassical grandeur. Olmsted had worked, if not with affinity, at least in courteous harmony with Beaux Arts architects like Hunt; indeed, he himself used formalistic elements in his work as he felt that symmetry and order were appropriate in the Central Park Mall and other promenades where large crowds were expected to congregate. Although he bitterly opposed the attempts to decorate his parks with a cake frosting of monumental entrances and archways, he made such concessions to the Beaux Arts spirit as he felt were warranted. In the site plan for the Columbian Exposition of 1893 in Chicago, he grouped the great white halls of his collaborators around a series of formal courts. It was the dazzling eclectic architecture of the Exposition that captured the public imagination and sent every major city in the country into a frenzy of municipal aggrandizement, eclipsing the unheroic, less self-conscious style that Olmsted had practiced for the preceding thirty-five years.

Now the pendulum has reversed. Monumental grandeur is no longer considered the hallmark of a sophisticated civilization. In the age of ecology the mood of a growing segment of the population is again one of appreciation of the role of nature in the urban context. Long neglected, Olmsted has gained a new relevancy and reputation as people are rediscovering the importance of his work and words.

The trail that I have followed in reconstructing Olmsted's aesthetic perceptions and social values has been blazed by historians; friends have helped me on my way. My primary debt of gratitude is to Charles McLaughlin, who, with the help of other Olmsted scholars, is editing a five-volume edition of the Olmsted papers and who generously provided me with a copy of his doctoral dissertation, "The Selected Letters of Frederick Law Olmsted."

Articles in various quarterlies and journals by Laura Wood Roper, author of a forthcoming biography of Frederick Law Olmsted, have been helpful, as have the collected reports relating to Olmsted's plans for New York, *Landscape into Cityscape*, edited by Albert Fein, the author of another Olmsted biography. I am grateful to Victoria Ranney for copies of the correspondence of the Olmsted family while they were residing in California.

Conversations with Jason Epstein have aided my understanding of Olmsted in the context of American history, as have the bibliographic references provided me by Peter Decker. Thanks are also due to Jon Alvah Peterson for his courtesy in allowing me to read his doctoral dissertation, "The Origins of the Comprehensive City Planning Ideal in the United States," and to Sam Bass Warner for sending me a copy of his lecture notes on "The Loss of Purpose in Urban Landscape Architecture."

I am appreciative of the encouragement of Julian Bach, my literary agent and a long-time admirer of Olmsted. My thanks go to Margaret Goldwater of the staff of the Olmsted Sesquicentennial Committee for many helpful favors and to William Alex, my collaborator on this book, for shared insights, ideas, and information.

ELIZABETH BARLOW

The Picturesque Tradition: Viewing Nature Through a Claude Glass

Edward interrupted her by saying, "You must not inquire too far, Marianne—remember, I have no knowledge in the picturesque, and I shall offend you by my ignorance and want of taste, if we come to particulars. I shall call hills steep, which ought to be bold; surfaces strange and uncouth, which ought to be irregular and rugged; and distant objects out of sight, which ought only to be indistinct through the soft medium of a hazy atmosphere. You must be satisfied with such admiration as I can honestly give. I call it a very fine country—the hills are steep, the woods seem full of fine timber, and the valley looks comfortable and snug—with rich meadows and several neat farm-houses scattered here and there. It easily answers my idea of a fine country, because it unites beauty with utility—and I dare say it is a picturesque one too, because you admire it; I can easily believe it to be full of rocks and promontories, grey moss and brushwood, but these are all lost on me. I know nothing of the picturesque."

Jane Austen, *Sense and Sensibility*

Olmsted was thirty-five when, with the architect Calvert Vaux, he submitted the winning entry in the design competition for Central Park. In a long, reminiscing letter that he wrote many years later to an old girl friend, Lizzy Baldwin Whitney, he

Drawing in William Gilpin's *Forest Scenery*, 1791.

suggested that the dilettantism of his youth had not been completely pointless but, rather, had acted as fertilizer for his late-blooming career in landscape architecture. He said that while still a boy he had discovered two books in the Hartford public library that informed his whole way of looking at nature and later became his professional touchstones. They were Sir Uvedale Price's *On the Picturesque* and William Gilpin's *Forest Scenery,* both written at the end of the eighteenth century, "which I esteem so much more than any published since, as stimulating the exercise of judgment in matters of my art, that I put them into the hands of my pupils as soon as they come into our office, saying, 'You are to read these seriously, as a student of law would read Blackstone.'"

Price had based his appreciation of nature on the study of painting. Railing against the smoothed out, rounded, regular forms favored by the English estate designer "Capability" Brown, he urged landscape "improvers" to consult "the authorities of those great artists who have most diligently studied the beauties of nature." He especially praised the naturalistic lyrical repose of Claude Lorrain, which he characterized as *beautiful;* Salvator Rosa was admired for his rugged, dramatic *picturesque* effects based on roughness, sudden variation, and irregularity. Putting it another way, Price found beauty embodied in the smooth flowing lines of a Grecian temple in its perfect state, while a temple in ruins, shrouded with moss and vines, exemplified the picturesque. A third category of landscape—the *sublime*—was typified by mountains, awesome and vast in scale, or a tumultuous sea.

Gilpin, vicar of Boldre in New-Forest, spent much time traveling through that English preserve analyzing the visual character of its landscapes. *Forest Scenery* contains a long discourse on the aesthetic properties of various species of trees. Gilpin found, for instance, that "the oak joins the idea of strength to beauty; while the ash rather joins the ideas of beauty, and elegance." He thought "no tree is better adapted to receive grand masses of light" than

View of Central Park, 1862.

the elm, but found the beech ugly in spite of its picturesque trunk whose bark "tempts the lover to make it the depository of his mistress's name."

Olmsted, too, came to look at trees not so much as a botanist or gardener would, but rather as the arboreal pallette of the landscape artist; their forms and tints were the stuff from which scenic effects were made. He took Gilpin's precepts for park scenery to heart and made them the cardinal principles of landscape composition in his parks. Indeed, the Vicar of Boldre might well have been describing Central or Prospect parks when he recommended "a varied surface—where the ground swells, and falls—where hanging lawns, screened with wood, are connected with valleys—and where one part is continually playing in contrast with another," or advised that in park structures rustic simplicity take precedence over "all the labored works of art," and the park's boundaries be secreted from view.

Gilpin supplied his readers with a series of warm-tinted oval vignettes illustrating idealized tree forms and landscape qualities. The Price-Gilpin manner of looking at nature according to the principles of painterly composition is symbolized by a device known as a Claude glass. Reputedly invented as an art aid by the painter Claude Lorrain, it was a convex, dark-toned glass that reflected landscapes in miniature, with "old master" tints and merging detail. It was popular with landscape painters and gentlemen travelers in the seventeenth and eighteenth centuries and was still used in the first half of the nineteenth century. The Claude glass, whether actual or simply metaphorical, typifies the perception of nature as scenes, vignettes, "art."

Like other educated travelers of his day, Olmsted carried as mental baggage an imaginary Claude glass and the standards of Price and Gilpin wherever he traveled. The extended carriage tours with his father and stepmother, which formed his happiest recollections of his early life, were, he said, "really tours in search of the picturesque." When he was twenty-two, his father sent him to inspect some family property near his uncle David Brook's farm in Cheshire, Connecticut. He and a hired hand stayed in a "shantee" on the place, chopping firewood in anticipation of winter when the family would return to go sledding. To his father in Hartford, he wrote:

> I found some of the most picturesque & sublime scenes I ever saw within a mile or two. The mountains are remarkably grand—& every few rods almost is a brook which winds about in the gorges—till it finds the most effective spot for a display—when [it] jumps off & comes tumbling & smashing through the rocks—over the side of the mountains in the most astonishing manner.

Six years later, having left the Staten Island farm his father had bought for him to go on a walking tour of England with his brother John and Charles Loring Brace, he assembled his impressions in *Walks and Talks of an American Farmer in England.* "There we were right in the midst of it!" he exclaimed.

> The country—and such a country!—green, dripping, glistening, gorgeous! We stood dumb-stricken by its loveliness, as from the bleak April and bare boughs we had left at home, broke upon us that English May—sunny, leafy, blooming May—in an English lane; with hedges, English hedges, hawthorn hedges, all in blossom; homely old farm houses, quaint stables, and haystacks; the old church spire over the distant trees; the mild sun beaming through the watery atmosphere, and all so quiet—the only sounds the hum of bees and the crisp grass-tearing of a silken-skinned, real (unimported) Hereford cow over the hedge.

Olmsted's enchantment with English pastoral scenery never wore off, and even after he returned home it remained for him a kind of yardstick for judging landscapes. Charles McLaughlin, the Olmsted scholar, has remarked that, because of Olmsted's predisposition to the pastoral, "it was a struggle [for him] to come to terms with western scenery. He could sense the grandeur of the Yosemite Valley, but was happier when the great cliffs were veiled in the mists of the early rainy season so that one could enjoy without distraction the lovely pastoral scenery of the valley floor."

In Gilpinesque fashion, Olmsted analyzed English trees, praising the copper beech, which, along with the Norway spruce, gave "a dark, ponderous tone" to the landscape. He also admired the English elm. Though it was not as fine a single tree as the American elm, he noted, it was "even more effective in masses, because thicker and better filled out in general outline."

Olmsted liked the way animals were consciously used as grace notes, embellishing English parkscapes. He was particularly struck by the deer park at Eton Hall, which he saw in the mellow light of late afternoon.

> Herds of fallow-deer, fawns, cattle, sheep and lambs quietly feeding near us, and moving slowly in masses at a distance; a warm atmosphere, descending sun and sublime shadows from fleecy clouds transiently darkening in succession, sunny surface, cool woodside, flocks and herds, and foliage.

Recollections of Eton Hall must have figured in his design of the sheep meadow in Central Park and the deer meadow in Prospect Park.

Not just the English landscape in general, but English parks, particularly those that followed the principles of the eighteenth-century landscape improver, Humphrey Repton, must have made a lasting impression on Olmsted, for Reptonian elements are to be found in his parks. Repton established a middle ground between the smoothed-out forms of "Capability" Brown and the unkempt naturalism recommended by the practitioners of the picturesque school. An early advocate of designing with nature, he believed that "all rational improvement of grounds is, necessarily, founded on a due attention to the *character* and *situation* of the place to be improved" and that "one of the fundamental principles of landscape gardening is to disguise the real boundary," precepts Olmsted followed in his designs.

A typical Repton composition included trees grouped in clumps upon a gently undulating greensward with grazing animals to give scale, intimate gardening effects being reserved for the immediate vicinity of the house. Picturesqueness could also be applied to such a scheme, but a Repton park, unlike those championed by the more radical followers of the picturesque, was meant to be practical as well as painterly.

The parks that Repton and his associate, the architect John Nash, designed in the second half of the eighteenth century were chiefly for private estates. Though some of these were later turned over to public use, the public park was a Victorian invention contemporary with the rise of the smoky industrial town. Olmsted had the opportunity when he was in England to visit one of the great early examples, Birkenhead outside Liverpool, the work of Joseph Paxton.

Birkenhead, opened in 1847, was Reptonian Picturesque in style. Earth had been moved to form little hills and valleys that were traversed by serpentine paths. Paxton's plan for Birkenhead included a belt of detached villas and terraces surrounding the park proper. The park had cost nearly £70,000 to build; however, this amount had been returned to the Improvement Commissioners by the incremental increase in the value of the villa lots that were then sold. This lesson was not lost on Olmsted, who was later to argue that a large increase in adjacent land values would inevitably result from well-planned parks, parkways, and suburban streets. Of his visit to Birkenhead, he wrote enthusiastically:

> Five minutes of admiration, and a few more spent in studying the manner in which art had been employed to obtain from nature so much beauty, and I was ready to admit that in democratic America, there was nothing to be thought of as comparable with this People's Garden. Indeed, gardening had here reached a perfection that I had never before dreamed of. I cannot undertake to describe the effect of so much taste and skill as had evidently been employed; I will only tell you, that we passed by winding paths over acres and acres, with a constant varying surface where on all sides were growing every variety of shrubs and flowers, with more

Sheep grazing in Prospect Park, 1914.

than natural grace, all set in borders of greenest, closest turf, and all kept with the most consummate neatness. . . .

But this is but a small part. Besides the cricket and an archery ground, large valleys were made verdant, extensive drives arranged—plantations, clumps, and avenues of trees formed, and a large park laid out. And all this magnificent pleasure-ground is entirely, unreservedly, and forever the people's own.

Memories of Birkenhead and the whole composite effect of English country scenery stimulated Olmsted's imagination when he conceived the plan for Central Park in 1858. Before that, however, his attention was turned in another direction.

Upon his arrival home, he found the country in political tur-moil over the 1850 Fugitive Slave Law requiring the return of runaway slaves to their rightful owners. His friend Charles Loring Brace tried to recruit Olmsted to the abolitionist cause. Brace finally decided that the best way to convince him was to make him see the South at firsthand. He thereupon commended Olmsted to Henry Jarvis Raymond, editor of the New York Times, who commissioned him to do a series of letters for the newspaper.

For the next fourteen months, Olmsted toured the South, and eventually his impressions, which first appeared in the Times under the signature "Yeoman," were collected and published as A Journey in the Seaboard Slave States, A Journey Through Texas (compiled and edited by John Olmsted from his brother's notes), and A Journey in the Back Country. The burden of Olm-sted's argument in these books rested less on the inhumanity of slavery than on its diseconomy. He constantly compared the cost of Northern agricultural production with Southern. He contended that slaves, whose only incentive was the overseer's whip, were much less efficient laborers than hired hands and self-employed farmers.

Throughout his Southern travels—all the while gathering facts, compiling statistics, reporting conversations—Olmsted managed to observe and criticize scenery. Embedded in his comments on slavery are remarkably sensitive descriptions of the American landscape as he saw it from train windows, steamboat decks, coach boxes, on mule and on horseback.

He loved the exoticism of the South Carolina bayous where the trees were festooned with Spanish moss "like a fringe of tangled hair, of a light gray pearly color, [which] sometimes produces exquisite effects when slightly veiling the dark green, purple and scarlet of the cedar, and the holly with their berries." In Kentucky, he found a beautiful countryside reminiscent of the deer park at Eton Hall.

Here spreads, for hundreds of miles before you, an immense natural park, planted, seeded to sward, drained, and kept up by invisible hands for the delight and service of man. Travel where you will for days, you find always the soft, smooth sod, shaded with oaks and beeches, noble in age and form, arranged in vistas and masses, stocked with herds, deer, and game. Man has squatted here and there over the fair heritage, amidst this luxuriant beauty of nature. It is landscape gardening on the largest scale. The eye cannot satiate itself in a whole day's swift panorama, so charmingly varied is the surface, and so perfect each new point of view.

The banks of the Mississippi were "a great wilderness of unexplored fertility, into which a few men have crept like ants

in a pantry." Though he passed caravans of immigrants, Texas was even more sparsely populated. There Olmsted was charmed by the sunny open prairies:

The live-oaks, standing alone or in picturesque groups near and far upon the clean sward, which rolled in long waves that took, on their various slopes, bright light or half shadows from the afternoon sun, contributed mainly to an effect which was very new and striking, though still natural, like a happy melody.

Frederick Law and John Hull Olmsted camping in Texas, 1854.

Botanizing in the Gilpin manner on his way back home through Mississippi, he observed

> frequent groves of magnolia grandiflora, large trees, and every one in the glory of full blossom. The magnolia does not, however, show well in masses, and those groves, not unfrequently met, were much finer, where the beech, elm, and liquidambar formed the body, and the magnolias stood singly out, magnificent chandeliers of fragrance.

Upon his return to New York, Olmsted, with $5,000 backing from his father, entered into partnership with the firm of Dix and Edwards, his publisher for the *Journey in the Seaboard Slave States*. The firm had recently purchased *Putnam's Monthly Magazine*, and Olmsted was asked to become the magazine's editor.

A pleasant by-product of Olmsted's new job, particularly after the fourteen months of weary evenings he had recently spent eating cornbread and bacon and trying to get a story out of his Southern hosts, was the life of witty socializing he now embarked upon. In the fall of 1855, William Makepeace Thackeray was visiting America, and Olmsted was undoubtedly present on at least one of the several occasions when the novelist was entertained at the Century Club. He also became a member of the Press Club and dined with Washington Irving at Astor House.

Throughout the spring and summer of 1856, Olmsted was in London trying to make arrangements to have Dix and Edwards publish English works in America on consignment. There he was entertained at Thackeray's with the editors of *Punch,* and he delighted in the way the English literati accomplished things, remarking that "under the vinous warmth the good things sprout." His pleasant, leisurely existence gave him plenty of time to indulge his favorite pastime, visiting the parks of London. As his publishing firm, unbeknown to Olmsted, was nearing bankruptcy, whose park strolls were ultimately the most productive feature of his stay. He later reminisced:

> In the six months that I was living in London, when in that miserable book business, I had no more idea of ever being a park-maker than of taking command of the channel fleet. But hardly a day passed in which I did not ramble in one a little. On holidays I went to Kew and Bushy and Richmond & Windsor. I [came] to look at public grounds critically but not at all from the official point of view or a gardener's point of view but from that of a citizen seeking rest, refreshment, recreation in [them]. So it happened that when Central Park was to be laid out & managed it is quite possible that I was more intimate with public parks and had a better understanding of what they should be than any other man of American birth and breeding.

Central Park

You are perfectly aware, as you hang about her in May and June, that you have, as a travelled person, beheld more remarkable scenery and communed with nature in ampler and fairer forms; but it is equally definite to you that none of those adventures have counted more to you for experience, for stirred sensibility—inasmuch as you can be, at the best, and in the showiest countries, only thrilled by the pastoral or the awful, and as to pass, in New York, from the discipline of the streets to this so different many-smiling presence is to be thrilled at every turn.

Henry James, *The American Scene*

It seems strange, in retrospect, that with his social and business connections and his already well-developed interest in scenic landscapes Olmsted had not taken from the beginning a more vigorous role in the campaign for a park for New York. As far back as 1844, when he was still a part-time student at Yale, William Cullen Bryant's *Evening Post* had editorialized in favor of a major natural park. Bryant had in mind a specific site, Jones Wood, the beautiful tract along the East River shore between 68th and 77th Streets, which, while it existed, was a pleasant waterfront haunt of anglers, picnickers, and solitude-seekers. Its uneven surface, with rocky outcroppings and sparkling streams, lent itself admirably to a picturesque landscape treatment. "Nothing is wanting," Bryant wrote, "but to cut winding paths through it, leaving the woods as they now are and introducing here and there a jet

from the Croton Aqueduct, the streams from which would make their own waterfalls over the rocks, and keep the brooks running through the place always fresh and full."

The Hudson River landscape gardener and tastemaker Andrew Jackson Downing in his magazine *The Horticulturist* also had taken up the subject of a park for New York. Visiting England in 1850, the same year Olmsted was there on his walking tour with his brother and Charles Brace, Downing was impressed with the parks of London. Pressing the tender nerve of his American readers' cultural inferiority complex, he wrote: "What are called parks in New York are not even apologies for the thing; they are only squares or paddocks." A year later Horace Greeley made the same trip and announced: "The parks, squares and public gardens of London beat us clear out of sight."

Downing and Greeley were right; the city with its population of 600,000 had scarcely 100 acres of park land. Washington Square and Madison Square, before they became parks, had served as potter's fields and had been used to bury the victims of the cholera epidemics that had periodically scourged the city. There was a handful of other residential squares—Tompkins, Union, Gramercy, and Mount Morris in Harlem. The only true parks as such were Bowling Green, City Hall Park, and Battery Park, which was built on landfill from nearby building excavations.

Through the editorializing of Bryant and Downing, the desirability of creating a large park in New York entered the public consciousness and became a political issue in the mayoralty campaign of 1850. Both candidates endorsed the park concept, and in 1851 the winner, Ambrose C. Kingland, issued a message to the Common Council calling for "the purchase and laying out of a park, on a scale which will be worthy of the city." With the concurrence of the Council, a bill was sent to Albany recommending Jones Wood as the most desirable site for a new park, and on July 11, 1851, legislation authorizing the taking of that property— 154 acres bounded by 66th and 75th Streets between Third Avenue and the East River—was passed.

There was immediate opposition to the bill from several quarters. The city's businessmen were aghast at the idea of forsaking potentially valuable commercial waterfrontage for such a frivolity. Downing, on the other hand, thought a 154-acre park ridiculously small to meet New York's future recreational needs. "It is only a child's playground!" he cried. "Five hundred acres is the smallest area that should be reserved for the future wants of such a city, *now*, while it may be obtained." He proposed a central reservation bordering the distributing reservoirs of the Croton Aqueduct. While Bryant felt that its beauties and waterfront location made Jones Wood a particularly apt choice for a park, he did not hold that it was the only suitable site; in fact, he thought it would be a fine idea if the public were to gain both Jones Wood and the central reservation.

A select committee of the state senate was appointed to consider the comparative merits of the two locations. Expert testimony was collected. The botanist John Torrey, who had frequented Jones Wood since boyhood, told the committee of its "fine specimens of oaks, tulip tree, liquidambar, hickories, birch, and some cedars," and he said he preferred Jones Wood to the "more bald and unpicturesque" central reservation. Others who appeared before the committee remarked on the rocky barrenness of the central reservation, since practically all the trees had been cut down when the Croton reservoir system was built. However, it was agreed that with a large expenditure for draining and topsoil and tree planting, it could become a beautiful park. Furthermore, it would increase the value of property surrounding it. After weighing what it had heard, the committee recommended that both parks be acquired, but urged that Jones Wood be developed first since its landscape attractions were immediate rather than long-range. With humane pragmatism, the authors of the report of the committee's findings argued:

> The panting and crowded families of the less wealthy, whose children fill the bills of mortality, are entitled to ask, what has posterity done for us? Why should they be taxed *now* to plant groves, which seventy years hence may shelter those who come after them, when health and pure air, wafted from the breezy river, through ample shades, are within their present grasp?

Acting on the advice of the report, the legislature in 1853 passed two bills, one authorizing Jones Wood, and the other Central Park, extending from 59th to 106th Streets between Fifth and Eighth Avenues. But, with the furor created by the commercial interests, the Jones Wood Act was repealed, and Manhattan lost its great opportunity for a major waterfront park on the East Side. But at least it could look forward to having in the future, after the expenditure of a large amount of money and labor, one large-scale public park.

A Board of Commissioners consisting of the Mayor and the Street Commissioner was established to guide the park's development with advice from a Consulting Board chaired by Washington Irving. Egbert Viele, who in 1853 had begun making a topographical survey and a general plan for the development of the new park lands in the hope that he could eventually receive "compensation suitable to the time and skill . . . expended on the work," was appointed chief engineer.

One thing was certain: if nothing else became of the new park, it was going to be a political football. Dapper, mustachioed Fernando Wood, Ambrose Kingland's opponent in the 1850 election, had become Mayor in 1854. Opponents of his Tammany-dominated administration, desiring to wrest from Wood the extensive opportunities for power and patronage that construction of the new park would provide, succeeded in getting Albany to pass a bill setting up an independent, theoretically nonpartisan, eleven-man commission in 1857. Viele was reappointed chief engineer by the new Board of Commissioners, but, not willing to give him carte blanche to carry out his development plans, the commission passed a resolution to hold a design competition. In the meantime, before any new plan was chosen, the work of the park, which at that stage was mostly a clearing operation, was to be carried out according to Viele's direction. As a large laboring force was to be employed, it would be necessary to hire a superintendent to oversee the men.

Sitting at a teatable at an inn by the Connecticut shore revising the manuscript of *A Journey in the Back Country*, his only occupation since the failure of his publishing firm, Olmsted chanced to meet Charles Wyllis Elliot, a close friend of Charles Loring Brace and now a member of the new commission overseeing Central Park. Elliot told Olmsted about the commission's intended appointment of a superintendent and urged him to apply for the position. Olmsted agreed and immediately set out to collect several signatures endorsing his candidacy, including those of such notables as Washington Irving, Peter Cooper, and Professor Asa Gray, the Harvard botanist.

Olmsted badly wanted the job. On September 11, 1857, while nervously waiting in the corridor outside the room where the commissioners were meeting to determine the outcome of his application, he wrote to his brother John, "I have moved to town and done nothing else since I last wrote but canvass for the Superintendent's office."

Originally the office was to have carried a salary of $3,000, with the superintendent's rank equal to Viele's, the engineer. This figure had subsequently been reduced to $1,500, and the superintendent made subordinate to the engineer. Olmsted said he had been "so foolish as to think of declining to take the office at that salary," but after "having had time to reflect, 'What else can I do for a living?'" had decided to press forward with his candidacy. He confided to John, "On the whole, as the times are, I shall think myself fortunate if I can earn $1,500. The times are worse and worse. The merchants and bankers horribly blue, and bank-riots are almost apprehended. The talk is much worse than you would suppose from the papers."

The plates and stock of *Putnam's Magazine* and Dix and Edwards were being liquidated and the proceeds turned over to creditors. Olmsted's erstwhile partners were in even more dire straits than he. Recently he had spotted Edwards "pale, nervous . . . and evidently *skinning,* in the streets," while Dix in slightly shabby clothing was going about distributing a card advertising himself as an insurance broker.

After a very lengthy session of the park board, Olmsted was informed that the commissioners had by a vote of eight to one awarded him the job in spite of their fears that he might be incompetent because he was a "literary man," not a "practical man." But, as he shrewdly observed to John, "If I had not been a 'literary man' so far, I certainly would not have stood a chance." One of the commissioners later confirmed that it had been the signature of Washington Irving—himself scarcely a "practical man"—on Olmsted's petition that had settled the case.

The park superintendency was Olmsted's baptism in the nefarious politics of mid-nineteenth-century New York. Fernando Wood had been reelected for a second term in 1856. His strength, like that of most of the Common Council, was based on an alliance with the city's most notorious element, such gangs as the Dead Rabbits and the Bowery Boys who provided muscle in ward politics. Using the financial panic and the general unemployment of 1857 as a pretext for enlarging his constituency by rabble-rousing methods, Wood urged the poor to seek jobs in the park. This in itself was not a bad idea, but it certainly portended a chaotic situation for the new superintendent.

The office in the park where Engineer Viele presided was literally besieged with thousands of applicants for jobs as park laborers. Each man bore a letter of recommendation, usually from a member of the Common Council. The councilmen, as politically unscrupulous as the Mayor, were in the habit of issuing such letters indiscriminately to all comers and then subsequently furnishing the engineer with a list of their true preferences, that is, those men who had earned high marks for their services in ward politics. If an applicant's name was found on the list, he was, without any other inquiry into his qualifications, given a job.

The political quagmire was matched by the appearance of the park itself, which was rubbish-strewn, deep in mud, filled with recently vacated squatters' huts, and overrun with goats left behind by the squatters. Until they were eventually impounded, the rampant goats were a great nuisance, eating the foliage of the park's few trees.

Had Andrew Jackson Downing survived the steamboat disaster that terminated his career as America's most influential landscape gardener in 1852, it is doubtful that there ever would have been a design competition for Central Park. In all likelihood, he would have been commissioned simply to plan the new park. Downing did, however, leave a successor, a young English architect named Calvert Vaux, whom he had taken into partnership in his Newburgh firm two years before he died. For a while after Downing's death, Vaux carried on the firm's practice, finishing up

commissions for estates that were already in progress on Long Island and along the Hudson. He then moved with his wife and young family to New York, intending to set up practice on his own.

It is not certain what led Vaux to propose collaboration in the design competition to Olmsted: perhaps because he was primarily an architect, even though he had acquired a good knowledge of gardening in Downing's office. The new park superintendent had a greater familiarity with the park's terrain than he. When Vaux first approached him, Olmsted refused for fear of offending Viele, who, since his original plan had been discarded, was planning to submit another himself. (Actually Viele merely resubmitted the same plan; he was completely convinced that his design could not be improved upon and would have been adopted already had "the right name" been appended to it.) On consideration, Olmsted decided to put the matter before Viele, and when Viele retorted contemptuously that it was a matter of complete indifference to him whether Olmsted entered or not, Olmsted immediately accepted Vaux's proposal.

With Olmsted's decision to participate in the competition, his critical viewing and classification of scenery according to the standards of Price and Gilpin, his accumulated knowledge of agriculture and botany, his desire to effect social amelioration through environmental improvements at last united with opportunity, and the long gestation period was over. Olmsted the artist was born. His birth certificate was the Greensward Plan, and Calvert Vaux's role in this event was that of midwife, for Vaux, with his training in architecture and his apprenticeship to Downing, could give Olmsted, who was still only a man of ideas, the skills necessary to turn ideas into plans.

Vaux gave Olmsted much more than mere technical education and assistance. Olmsted always insisted that Vaux's own artistry in planning Central Park be recognized. Throughout the years of partnership that followed, Vaux was the steady anchor that the high-strung Olmsted with his strong competing interests needed, for Vaux more than anyone else comprehended Olmsted's innate artistic talents. Eight years later, when Olmsted was in California as manager of the Mariposa mines, it was Vaux's persuasive appeals that steered him back into a career of landscape architecture. Now it was his inspiration and collaboration that made it possible for Olmsted to realize the greatest opportunity of his life.

For the next five months, Olmsted worked at an unremitting pace. Besides carrying out his duties in the park (he confidently announced to his father, "I have got the park into a capital discipline, a machine 1,000 men now at work"), every free moment on evenings and Sundays was spent discussing the park design with Vaux. During the days as he made his rounds, he was constantly analyzing the park's terrain, regarding it as a sculptor would his marble or a painter his canvas, and at night he and Vaux would pace over its acres in the moonlight, arguing out each feature of their plan. Gradually a vision began to form. By judiciously clearing away here and planting there, by moving earth to rearrange the land into more pleasing contours, by laying drains and converting swamps into ponds, there would emerge a landscape that was at once naturalistic and picturesque.

Eventually it was time to sit down at the drafting table in Vaux's house at 136 East 18th Street and render their ideas on paper. Downing Vaux, who was a little boy at the time, was to remember Olmsted and his father hard at work getting their design ready for submission. "There was," he said, "a great deal of grass to be put in by the usual small dots and dashes, and it became the friendly thing for callers to help in the work by joining in and 'adding some grass to Central Park.'" Perhaps the trouble expended on drawing so much grass prompted the designers to sign their plan "Greensward." On April 1, 1858, the last day of the competition, Olmsted and Vaux delivered "Greensward," which was labeled number 33, out of thirty-five entries, to the park board (Ills. 15–23).

More than any of the other designs, number 33 embodied a thoughtful prognosis of the future needs of the city. The name Central Park had been chosen because the site for the park was the central reservation, not Jones Wood on the East River. Olmsted and Vaux chose to put a different interpretation on the name of the park. They envisioned the day when it would be the unbuilt-upon center of a large, teeming population, when all the natural scenery existing outside of the park was erased and it would be the central experience of nature for the majority of residents of a huge metropolis. Prophetically Olmsted wrote:

> The time will come when New York will be built up, when all the grading and filling will be done, and when the picturesquely varied, rocky formations of the Island will have been converted into formations for rows of monotonous straight streets, and piles of erect buildings. There will be no suggestion left of its present varied surface, with the single exception of the few acres contained in the Park. Then the priceless value of the present picturesque outlines of the ground will be perceived, and its adaptability for its purpose more fully recognized.

The park that Olmsted and Vaux envisioned as an antidote to this ubiquitous urban mass was to offer a "constant suggestion to the imagination of an unlimited range of rural conditions," an artful blend of pastoral and woodland scenery. Every suggestion of the city was to be screened out; trees were to be planted in such a way as to "leave uncertainty as to the occupation of the space beyond, and establish a horizon line, composed as much as possible of verdure."

The collaborators had from the first recognized that the

park's long, narrow rectangular shape militated against their aims. In order to provide the desired "umbrageous horizon line" and screen out the buildings that were soon to spring up around the park's periphery, the Greensward Plan called for a line of trees all around the outside of the park between the sidewalk and the street.

Another problem posed by the shape of the park was the necessity of having four east-west crossings. It is not certain whether Olmsted and Vaux were familiar with the underpass that had been built in the Regent's Park Zoo in 1850; it would have been unlikely, however, for Olmsted in all his rambles in London parks during his extended business trip in 1856 to have missed it. In any case, the underpass, or sunken transverse road, was a brilliant solution to keeping all the hurly-burly of "coal carts and butchers' carts, dust carts and dung carts," the inevitable and

Central Park Transverse Road, 1860.

legitimate traffic of a busy city, from intruding upon the park experience, annihilating a visitor's impression of "an unlimited range of rural conditions."

The park would contain, in all, four separate traffic systems: (1) the long, sweeping east and west drives for hackney coaches and carriages; (2) the bridle trail circling the reservoir and meandering elsewhere through the park, always carried by means of an underpass beneath carriage and pedestrian crossings; (3) a system of footpaths generally following the carriage drives "so that pedestrians may have ample opportunity to look at the equipages and their inmates"; and (4) depressed and made as unobtrusive as possible, the four sunken thoroughfares.

The park's northern end, which in the beginning was terminated by 106th Street (a mistake that was remedied at considerable expense five years later, when it became apparent that the craggy terrain immediately north of 106th Street was unsuitable for development, and the park was extended to a more logical boundary at 110th Street), was admirably suited to a picturesque landscape treatment. Since the views in this section of the park are more sweeping than in the southern half, Olmsted and Vaux felt that here a unity of treatment should prevail throughout and "formal and architectural effects, unless on a very grand scale, must be avoided."

By contrast, the southern half of the park, which has more interrupted views, lent itself to a greater diversity of effects. Being closer to the main point of entry into the park, it would receive the most concentrated use. Here it would be appropriate to break away from the carefully orchestrated passages of naturalistic scenery—gleaming, smooth meadow turf in counterpoint to rocky, forested heights—and introduce a purely formalistic element reminiscent of the grand boulevards of Paris. However, in keeping with the spirit of the park, the visual terminus of this avenue should be scenic, not architectural; it should lead the visitor away from the sights and sounds of the city to something deep within the heart of the park. The promenade or Grand Mall was therefore positioned on a diagonal to the park's boundaries, with its scenic focal point Vista Rock, the highest point in the park. This promontory was to be accentuated, but not overemphasized, by a small architectural feature, the Belvedere Castle. Indeed, by keeping the Belvedere somewhat dwarfish in scale, the impression from the Mall of gazing across a great distance was enhanced.

In its original state, the park had several swamp-bordered brooks running through it, but Olmsted and Vaux felt that "mere rivulets are uninteresting, and we have preferred to collect the ornamental water in large sheets, and carry off through underground drains the water that at present runs through the park in shallow brooks." And so the lakes in Central Park, which today seem so natural and unpremeditated in their outlines, were created by excavating and installing a system of drainage pipes a total of 95 miles in length to carry off excess surface water and to allow for periodic infusions of fresh water from the reservoir.

Besides the irregularly shaped reservoir with which we are familiar today, there was at the park's inception a rectangular receiving reservoir, later converted into the Great Lawn. Like the strict, straight boundaries of the park itself, this reservoir was a design impediment which Olmsted and Vaux successfully minimized by banking its walls with trees and carrying the carriage drives away from it.

Above all, the Greensward designers believed in one overriding principle—the integrity of the park as a whole. Like a symphony, it would have a clearly stated and recurring theme, rural scenery, and whatever modulations occurred would be subservient to this central theme. Olmsted wrote: "The Park throughout is a single work of art, and as such subject to the primary law of every work of art, namely that it shall be framed upon a single, noble motive, to which the design of all the parts, in some more or less subtle way, shall be confluent and helpful." A few buildings, low in profile and unobtrusive in design, sited on the park's boundary or beside one of the transverse roads, and an incidental bold architectural effect like the Mall, carefully positioned with reference to a particular scenic attraction, were admissible. Olmsted and Vaux were yet to learn how perilously vulnerable to a host of encroachments the park would be, especially during the disastrous days of the early 1870's, when it fell into the hands of the Tweed ring and its vacant acres were considered solely as sites for public works projects that would fill the pockets of Tammany commissioners with graft money.

For four weeks after the submission of the designs, the park board deliberated until, on April 28, by a vote of seven to four, the first prize was awarded to plan number 33. Some of the commissioners felt that even after the selection of a winner the board should still be free to pick and choose ideas from among the various entries. Robert J. Dillon and August Belmont mounted the principal attack on the Greensward Plan. On June 8, 1858, the T.ibune ran their counterproposal: a grand Champs-Elysée type of boulevard going from 59th Street to the south wall of the old reservoir. This great formal thoroughfare bisecting the park would be carried over the lake at 73rd Street by a wire suspension bridge. The big square reservoir, which Olmsted and Vaux's plan attempted to hide, was admired in its day as a feat of hydraulic engineering. In Dillon's and Belmont's eyes, it was the crowning glory of the park and should be apotheosized with "a flight of marble steps upon a marble platform in front of the wall."

The *Tribune* editorialized in favor of the Dillon-Belmont proposal, calling it "the perfection of common sense," whereupon Olmsted promptly invited Charles Dana, the *Tribune*'s city editor, and Henry Raymond of the *Times* to have breakfast with him in the park. He later explained: "I seated them at table in a tent set on a grand rock in the Ramble right on the line of the proposed avenue. When they were smoking I asked them to look southward and consider what destruction even of existing natural beauty; what excessive belittling of the already too petty scenery, the proposition meant. They at once both confessed that they had not realized its import, and if they did not both come out against it publicly, they at least ceased to favor it. It was a case of natural eloquence versus grandiloquence."

Dillon and Belmont also objected to the four transverse roads, which they proposed to abolish entirely since "there will be little or no such business relations of one side with the other as to require vehicles of traffic to cross the Park." A committee was appointed to settle the matter, and, after conferring with Olmsted, who made certain minor concessions but gained a victory for maintaining the plan intact, it was resolved "that the Superintendent be required to proceed forthwith to form working plans for the construction of the Park, and to stake out the principal features upon the ground." The superintendent was also authorized to enlist the services of his associate Vaux and to employ up to six assistants.

The superaddition of authority to the superintendent naturally left the chief engineer in an ambiguous, if not untenable, position. Clearly the work in the park would have to proceed along lines dictated by Olmsted, not Viele, The park board realized this, and at their next meeting they resolved to dismiss Viele and raise Olmsted's salary to $2,500 a year, appointing him architect-in-chief, an office that subsumed both the powers that Viele had previously held and the duties of the superintendent.

There is a photograph of Olmsted in a cape and military-style visored cap taken during the initial period of park building (Ill. 12). It shows how he must have looked patrolling the park like an army general conveying orders to his lieutenants, the supervisors overseeing the laying of drains for the ponds, the

grubbing and tilling of the park's soil, and the blasting, excavating, and grading of portions of its rocky, irregular surface. The architect-in-chief appears to wear his authority confidently; the pale, clear eyes are fixed on the distance, a slightly drooping mustache and soft curls frame a resolutely set jaw. Though slight of build, he cuts a rather imposing figure, radiating purposefulness and an altogether imperious will.

Because the ranks of the unemployed were swollen with thousands of would-be laborers encouraged by Tammany politicians to look on the new park as an immense public-relief project, for Olmsted it was not simply a matter of recruiting and overseeing a workforce adequate to implement his plans. According to him, "It was a general impression that the pretense of work was merely a form of distributing the public money to the poor and my office was for several days regularly surrounded by an organized mob carrying a banner inscribed 'Bread and Blood.' This mob sent in to me a list of 10,000 names of men alleged to have starving families, demanding that they should be immediately put at work." The portrait that Olmsted drew of himself as an administrator shows him as somewhat of a martinet, keeping the workforce "economically employed and rigidly discharging any man who failed to work industriously and behave in a quiet, orderly manner."

Temperamental and autocratic by nature, he was at this period under a severe nervous strain. His amiable younger brother John, his best friend and companion on the walking tour of England and the journey to Texas, had recently died of tuberculosis. More out of a sense of duty than anything else, he married John's widow, Mary, a strong-willed, ambitious woman, and thereby became the stepfather to John and Mary's three children. The summer of 1859 was stifling, and Olmsted, overworked in his efforts to get the park construction launched, succumbed to intermittent fevers. In the fall he took a leave of absence to study the parks of England. As always, he was cheered by the sight of the gentle English countryside he admired so much. In 1856 he had walked in the London parks for his own pleasure and amusement, but now he looked at them with a professional eye, questioning their superintendents and collecting a body of useful information on their engineering, design, and maintenance. He also went to Paris, where he was introduced to Edouard Alphand, minister of roads and bridges, and the designer of the Bois de Boulogne and other parks outside Paris.

He told the Central Park commissioners that he returned "with greatly improved health, and with a satisfaction in my duty increased by a contemplation of the finished work abroad." He also found that he was to be a father. On June 14, 1860, a son, John Theodore, was born. Tragically, the child died two months later from cholera. Olmsted himself suffered a carriage accident at about this time in which he fractured his thigh in three places, an injury that left him with a game leg for years. Soon, however, he was being carried around the park in a litter, as, Pygmalion-like, he continued to woo its barren acres into art and life.

Over the years, hundreds of thousands of cart loads of rocks and glacial till—a legacy of the great ice sheet that had once covered Manhattan—were carried away or repositioned in the park, and hundreds of thousands of cubic yards of topsoil were brought in and spread over its surface. All the blasting and laborious hauling and earth-moving in those pre-bulldozer days was, as Olmsted observed, only the priming of the canvas upon which the landscape artist would paint picturesque scenes, the full outlines of which might not be realized for a generation. As he was to point out in one of several letters of resignation prompted by what he felt was interference with his role as architect-in-chief by the park's comptroller, Andrew Haswell Green,

the work of design necessarily supposes a gallery of mental pictures, and in all parts of the park I constantly have before me, more or less distinctly, more or less vaguely, a picture, which as Superintendent I am constantly laboring to realize. Necessarily the crude maps which are laid before you are but the merest hints of the more rigid outlines of these pictures, these plans.

I shall venture to assume to myself the title of artist . . . and to add that no sculptor, painter or architect can have anything like the difficulty in sketching and conveying a knowledge of his design to those who employ him which must attend upon an artist employed for such a kind of designing as is required of me. The design must be exclusively in my imagination.

In other words, the Greensward Plan was not a static document, but a creative process, and Olmsted felt his superintendency was absolutely vital to its successful outcome.

For Olmsted, recreation and the contemplation of scenery were synonymous; he felt that the pastoral beauty of the park would bring refinement and happiness to the city's inhabitants.

It is not simply to give the people of the city an opportunity for getting fresh air and exercise; . . . It is not simply to make a place of amusement or for the gratification of curiosity or for gaining knowledge. The main object and justification [of the park] is simply to produce a certain influence in the minds of people and through this to make life in the city healthier and happier. The character of this influence is a poetic one and it is to be produced by means of scenes, through observation of which the mind may be more or less lifted out of moods and habits into which it is, under the ordinary conditions of life in the city, likely to fall.

In 1861, however, Americans were less concerned with civilizing their cities than they were with the inexorably mounting tensions of civil strife.

Civil War Interlude

On April 24, 1861, twelve days after the firing on Fort Sumter, a resolution was passed by the New York County Board of Supervisors urging that all public works including the park be suspended "so far as may be warranted by a proper regard for the public interest." The park commissioners met and framed a letter of reply in which they pointed out that to dismiss the park's work force at a time of low employment would be "peculiarly onerous." It would also be very uneconomical to abandon the various park structures that were already half-constructed. In short, the board felt this was not "a time for public bodies to manifest a greater degree of timorousness and apprehension than has yet been shown by businessmen in their affairs."

Olmsted, prevented from enlisting for military duty because of his bad leg and generally delicate health, nevertheless wanted to work for the Union cause. His strained relations with Green, which had caused him to offer his resignation from his park duties the previous January, were no better in June. Thus, when the officers of the newly formed Sanitary Commission, realizing Olmsted's superior abilities as an administrator, offered him the post of executive secretary, he accepted. Moving nurses and supplies to the front would not be unlike moving men and materials in the park. He thereupon secured a leave of absence, and Vaux was appointed to take his place.

One of his first duties for the Sanitary Commission was to inspect the camps near Washington. The boys recruited to wear the Union blue were not hardened soldiers but youths fresh from the care of their mothers and wives, accustomed to a relatively high standard of living. Olmsted found that, without the means to bathe and wash their clothes, they soon became disheveled, lousy, and ragged. The states were expected to outfit their own regiments, but this proved difficult and very expensive as there was profiteering on wool, and the failure of the indigo crop in India sent the cost of blue dye soaring. The soldiers in the field often were in tatters, while new uniforms were hoarded at recruitment points as a sartorial inducement to volunteers.

Most camp sites were poorly laid out from a sanitary point of view. Drainage systems were inadequate, consisting of haphazard troughs that allowed water to collect and stagnate. Toilet facilities were rudimentary trenches often too near the camp site and so filthy and noisome the men refused to use them. As deadly as bullets were typhus, malaria, and scurvy.

In the beginning of the war, there were no general hospitals to receive the sick and wounded. In Washington, old government buildings without running water and toilets, and so poorly ventilated they became "storehouses for morbid emanations," were converted to medical use. But the greatest stumbling block faced by the Sanitary Commission was the ossified structure of the Medical Bureau itself, which the diarist George Templeton Strong, a member of the commission, characterized as "the most narrow, hidebound, fossilized, red-tape-y of all the departments in Washington." The Bureau operated under the rule of seniority, and according to Strong, "The fogies of that department manage it in the spirit of a village apothecary."

Strong assisted Olmsted in drafting a "Report to the Secretary of War." The report made recommendations concerning dress, diet, field hygiene, and sanitation, as well as suggestions for better administrative procedures within the Medical Bureau itself. It proposed that knapsacks be provided with combs and other toilet articles and that a company fund be set up to supplement the soldiers' ration of stale bacon and hardtack with fresh vegetables, butter, milk, and pepper. As a result of lobbying on the part of Olmsted and members of the Sanitary Commission, a bill was passed reorganizing the Medical Bureau, and William Hammond, a man sympathetic to the commission's views, was appointed Surgeon General.

Besides reforming the Medical Bureau and distributing the huge stream of food and goods that had been collected and forwarded to Washington from Sanitary Commission branches in the North, Olmsted took charge of the hospital transport service, evacuating wounded and sick soldiers from the York and James rivers following General McClellan's futile Peninsular Campaign.

Katherine Prescott Wormeley, a writer and volunteer nurse aboard the transport vessel that was Olmsted's headquarters, penned the following portrait of her "chief."

His face is generally very placid, with all the expressive delicacy of a woman's, and would be beautiful were it not for an expression which I cannot fathom,—something which is, perhaps, a little too severe about it. I think his mouth and smile and the expression of his eyes at times very beautiful. He has great variety of expression: sometimes stern, thoughtful, and haggard: at other times observing and slightly satirical (I believe he sees out of the back of his head occasionally); and then again, and not seldom, his face wears an inspired look, full of goodness and power. I think he is a man of the most resolute self-will,—generally a very wise will, I should think; born an autocrat, however, and, as such, very satisfactory to be under. His reticence is one of his strong points: he directs everything in the fewest possible words; there is a deep, calm thoughtfulness about him which is always attractive and sometimes—provoking.

The Battle of Fair Oaks sent a torrent of 3,000 wounded to the army base at White House. Olmsted was horrified at the sight of them, "packed as closely as they could be in freight cars . . . dead and living together in the same close box, many with awful wounds festering and swarming with maggots." Although technically only in charge of the offshore hospital transport ships, he pitched a tent beside the railroad track where the trains disgorged their terrible cargoes. His assistants warmed huge kettles of soup and tea for the trains that kept arriving all night.

The army medical authorities were continually imposing on Olmsted, using his Sanitary Commission transport ships as auxiliary regimental hospitals. Miss Wormeley fretted over the way Olmsted drove himself to the point of nervous exhaustion: "Mr. Olmsted's health begins to give the doctors serious uneasiness—so they tell me; but he says he is well." He thought he could hold out until the longed-for capture of Richmond, but agonized over what he would do when that anticipated battle sent down "a great avalanche of suffering" upon him. He and his assistant in charge of supplies, Frederick Knapp, now went "day and night without sleep, sometimes without food . . . working their physical strength to the utmost." Knapp eventually collapsed, a victim of typhoid, but Olmsted, haggard and still painfully lame from his carriage accident, persisted. His wife urged him to take a vacation, but he found the suggestion unthinkable and wrote her, "It is a day for heroes and we must be heroes with the rest."

In January, 1863, Strong found him "in an unhappy, sick, sore mental state. . . . Perhaps his most insanitary habits of life make him morally morbid. He works like a dog all day and sits up nearly all night, doesn't go home to his family (now established in Washington) for five days and nights together, works with steady, feverish intensity till four in the morning, sleeps on a sofa in his clothes, and breakfasts on *strong coffee and pickles!*

"It will be a terrible blow to the Commission if we have to throw Olmsted over. We could hardly replace him." Yet Strong feared that

> Olmsted is mismanaging our Sanitary Commission affairs. He is an extraordinary fellow, decidedly the most remarkable specimen of human nature with whom I have ever been brought into close relations. Talent and energy most rare; absolute purity and disinterestedness. Prominent defects, a monomania for system and organization on paper (elaborate, laboriously thought out, and generally impracticable), and appetite for power. He is a lay-Hildebrand.

Olmsted's position with the Sanitary Commission had obviously grown untenable, and he had little choice but to resign. In addition, he and Vaux had been forced to resign their Central Park commission because of political pressure. He wrote to his father at the time: "Vaux has been finally badgered off the park and my relations with it are finally closed. We couldn't bear it even as consulting architects."

In broken health from his Sanitary Commission exertions and still burdened with his old Dix and Edwards publishing debt, Olmsted needed two things—money and a complete change of scene. Miraculously, an offer combining both came to him in the summer of 1863. A group of New York investors had bought the Mariposa Mines, John C. Frémont's old estate in California. They needed a resident manager, and the job paid $10,000 plus $100,000 in stock. The disillusioning fact that the Mariposa estate was at the wrong end of the mother lode to be mined profitably had not yet become apparent. The investors had been duped; the previous managing agent and part-owner had shrewdly concentrated operations in only the richest seams, temporarily boosting profits in the months immediately prior to the offer of sale. As in the Dix and Edwards venture, Olmsted was to be an unwitting party to prospective financial disaster. Here the important distinctions were his personal lack of financial liability and, of course, the generous salary. He and his family could live very handsomely on $5,000 a year; with the additional $5,000, he could pay off his old debts and begin to build up his own estate.

Before departing for California, Olmsted went to Cambridge to see Charles Eliot Norton in an effort to raise money to start a new magazine, *The Nation.* The two men had never met before, although Norton had a tremendous admiration for Olmsted's Southern journals and had pronounced them "chief materials for our social history whenever it is written" (as indeed they have been). He said of Olmsted:

> I wish I had known him before he was just going to leave this quarter of the world. It is hard that he should have to give up the civilization that he likes for the barbarism that he does not like. All the lines of his face imply refinement and sensibility to such a degree that it is not till one has looked through them to what is underneath, that the force of his will and the reserved power of his character become evident. It is a pity that we cannot keep him here. Our society needs organizers as much as the Mariposa settlers, miners, and squatters need one.

With his journey to California, the tensions from the last months with the Sanitary Commission seemed to disappear, and the artistic side of his personality reemerged. Traveling through the Isthmus of Panama, Olmsted was fascinated with the fecundity of the tropics, "the superabundant creative power, infinite resource, and liberality of Nature—the childish playfulness and profuse careless utterance." From the Chagres River, he wrote to his wife, who was to follow him to California the next spring:

Remember to point out the mountains to the children and tell them they are the Andes. There are great vultures and pelicans floating about. There are light (thunder) showers (without the thunder) every hour or two. The passing veils of the showers and the outbursting sunshafts add to the dizzy gorgeousness of the foliage. It has excited me very much. . . . I am thoroughly enchanted with the trees and vines. But cane and palms are not trees or vines or shrubs or herbs. They are Gloria in Excelsis with lots of exclamation points, thrown in anywhere, in the grand choral liturgy.

The arid California landscape came as a shocking contrast to the dazzling Central American rain forest, and Olmsted, with his predisposition for pastoral and picturesque verdure was repulsed at first. He wrote his wife, "the whole aspect of the country is detestable . . . a region possessing less fertility—less of living nature you scarce ever saw. The style is Cyclopian, but the vegetation Lilliputian." However, his natural curiosity and background as a traveling journalist caused him immediately to begin collecting and revising his impressions. Not unexpectedly, his greatest praise was for landscapes that were evocative of familiar scenery; the Mariposa estate at twilight "when the ground appeared all the same as turf, and the vegetable productions, as trees," or Yosemite Valley when a midsummer haze gave it "an indescribable softness and exquisite dreamy charm . . . like that produced by the Indian summer of the East."

The California in which the Olmsteds planned to install themselves in civilized comfort (he had hired a French valet to attend him, and she would bring an English governess for the children) was still a raw, rambunctious frontier. The population was polyglot, the life lawless. Each ship entering San Francisco Bay brought more adventurers in search of gold. In every valley boasting the tiniest stream, Olmsted noticed Chinamen panning or industriously turning a treadmill to pump additional gold wash water out of the ground. The Homestead Act had only been passed one year before, and in California a stable agricultural population of Jeffersonian yeomen was yet a decade or so away.

Interestingly, it was in this milieu of transient fortune-hunters that Olmsted began to formulate the sociological theories that later blossomed into a philosophy of urban planning. He never believed in the myth of the western hero, the self-sufficient loner pitting his wits against nature, and the cupidity of hostile forces. For him, human happiness meant communality, interdependence, vocational specialization. He felt aggregate enterprise was more efficient and desirable than individualism in supplying a decent standard of living. Organized, civilized communities were morally preferable in his eyes to the wilderness ethic of ingenious survival. He deplored the absentee ownership of wealth he found in California and argued in his *Preliminary Report in Regard to a Plan of Public Pleasure Grounds for the City of San Francisco* (1866) for such civilizing amenities as would attract a permanent population.

California gave him another opportunity to construct a philosophy of land use for the public good. In 1865, he was appointed by Governor Frederick Low to head a commission to make recommendations on the management of Yosemite as a public preserve. Though it had first been seen by a white man only sixteen years before, Yosemite was already something of a tourist attraction frequented by several hundred visitors annually, and Congress

Frederick Law and Mary Olmsted
in the Yosemite Valley.

pursuit of happiness against the obstacles, otherwise insurmountable, which the selfishness of individuals or combinations of individuals is liable to interpose to that pursuit." And for Olmsted, one aspect of the pursuit of happiness, providing both moral and physical refreshment, was the contemplation of "natural scenes of impressive character.'"

But Olmsted had a pragmatic side as well, and as a believer in commercial progress he urged the preservation of Yosemite on economic grounds. The dollars lost in not mining or logging the site would be splendidly offset when it became a well-developed tourist attraction serviced by inns, railroads, and telegraph lines. One can hardly resist imagining what his horrified reaction would be if he could see today's valley campers with their automobiles and transistor radios in this once-tranquil sylvan setting.

Olmsted's expanding landscape tastes embraced more aspects of California than those which, like Yosemite, recalled English, alpine, or eastern United States scenery. He came to appreciate an intimate-scale gardenesque style of beauty, and he began to see how certain southern European building forms could be appropriated to its climate, vegetation, and topography. The house plans he recommended his wife have drawn up show Olmsted's instinct for harmonizing architecture with the land. To minimize the discomfort of the heat, they would locate on a hilltop; the house would be of native materials, built around a courtyard, and "have deep piazzas or galleries with low shades" to compensate for the lack of surrounding trees. It would look "as if knocked up by some mountaineer with a genius, and an axe and steam saw mill."

While architectonic western landscapes were innately less congenial to his romantic temperament than verdant pastoral ones, he had a sense of propriety, of fitness, of the *genius loci,* so that when he was commissioned in the fall of 1864 to lay out the Mountain View Cemetery in Oakland, he did not design it in the

had the previous year withdrawn it from the public domain and deeded it to the state of California "for public use, resort, and recreation," the first area in the nation to be set aside for such purpose.

Olmsted camped with his family on two occasions in the future national park. His preliminary report on *The Yosemite Valley and the Mariposa Big Trees* is a landmark document enunciating the individual's right to enjoy public scenery and the government's obligation to protect him in the exercise of that right. In language intentionally evocative of Jefferson, Olmsted wrote: "It is the main duty of government, if it is not the sole duty of government, to provide means of protection for all its citizens in the picturesque style. A lesser artist, given the same personal bias, would have tried to make it arcadian in the manner of Greenwood Cemetery in Brooklyn. It is a measure of the breadth of Olmsted's imagination and the depth of his talent that he did not. He chose, rather, a plan of formal simplicity resembling a Mediterranean villa garden and using native plant materials that would not require extensive watering during the dry season.

In another commission, the village and grounds for the College of California at Berkeley, he did revert to a picturesque treatment by specifying curvilinear streets to conform with topography, rather than a more formal plan. Here he was influenced by the pioneer suburb of Llewelyn, New Jersey, laid out by the architect Alexander Jackson Davis in 1853, but he adapted his plan to the California climate by advising the use of drought-resistant plants and the construction of houses designed for outdoor living.

At this period of his life, Olmsted still considered landscape design merely as a sideline. Even when it became obvious that the Mariposa mining venture was doomed, he did not think of devoting himself entirely to this type of work, although he obviously enjoyed it immensely. Rather, he considered returning to a life of journalism and tried unsuccessfully to buy a San Francisco newspaper, which he hoped his friend Edwin Lawrence Godkin would come out and edit. Godkin, however, had managed at last to raise the necessary capital to launch *The Nation*, the project on which Olmsted had been working on the eve of his departure to California. He urged Olmsted to return to New York and help him with the new magazine. At the same time, Vaux wrote Olmsted saying that they had been offered reappointment as landscape architects in Central Park and that there was another important commission awaiting collaboration: Prospect Park in Brooklyn.

Prospect Park

In 1859, when Olmsted was overseeing the initial stages of Central Park's construction, Brooklyn made its bid for a similarly large pleasure ground. A bill authorizing a park was passed by the state legislature that year, but the Civil War prevented the Brooklyn park commissioners from carrying out work other than designating boundaries and awarding compensation for the park's original 350 acres straddling Flatbush Avenue.

In 1861 Egbert Viele, the ex-engineer of Central Park, who had been rebuffed when Olmsted was appointed to supersede him, submitted *A Plan for the Improvement of Prospect Park*. The name of the park derived from Mount Prospect, the high hill at the intersection of Flatbush Avenue and what later became Eastern Parkway, on which was located the reservoir. The park that Viele would have built consisted of two lozenge-shaped parcels connected by overpasses across Flatbush Avenue and bore the same rather amateurish stamp as his scheme for Central Park (Ill. 93).

Though Viele was sanguine about the bisected park plan, some of the commissioners apparently were not. Calvert Vaux was called in to survey the park grounds and make suggestions for redefining its boundaries. He was immediately struck by the awkwardness of the original site and proposed that the eastern portion of the park be sold off and the proceeds used to acquire more land to the west. More than a mere amplification of acreage, the additional land would greatly increase the park visitor's illusion of space by making possible long, sweeping vistas. Instead of Mount Prospect, there would be Vanderbilt Hill, another fine van-

tage point with panoramic views across the farming hamlets of southern Brooklyn to New York Bay. On a wet Saturday in early January, 1865, Vaux walked with James Stranahan, the park board's president, over the proposed additional acres. He pointed out an extensive tract of low-lying land below Vanderbilt Hill that could be excavated for a large lake. The immediate and immense popularity of skating in Central Park indicated the desirability of having a really substantial sheet of water of fifty or sixty acres for this purpose. Civic rivalry between New York and Brooklyn was then at its zenith; the creation of such a lake would give the Brooklyn commissioners an opportunity to upstage their competitors in Central Park.

Unlike Andrew Haswell Green, the comptroller of Central Park, Stranahan always saw his relationship with Vaux, and later Olmsted, as that of client, rather than watchdog. He and his fellow commissioners maintained a receptivity and respect for the ideas of the landscape architects that would make the design of Prospect Park much freer from interference and argumentation than Central Park. At the outset, however, Vaux was still wary. He wrote Olmsted in California, "I really, however, approach the subject with a feeling akin to dislike, fearing to be annoyed as we were in the C P affair."

Vaux drew up an initial report on boundaries; appended to it was a diagram of the rearranged site showing a rough disposition of the park into three main elements: lake, rugged woodland, and an extensive rolling meadow (Ill. 92). Refined, this sketch plan became the basic blueprint for Prospect Park; so it can be argued that Vaux, not Olmsted, was its creator. Vaux, however, did not wish to proceed independently and wrote Olmsted repeatedly, urging him to return to New York. Recalling their collaboration on Central Park, he said:

> If you had been disheartened there very likely might have been no park to chatter about today, for I alone was wholly incompetent to take it up. . . . I had no idea of competing because I felt my incapacity;—I feel it no less—I will not say *no* less, but very little less;—now, and enter on Brooklyn alone with hesitation and distrust, not on the roads and walks or even planting . . . but in regard to the main point,— the translation of the republican art idea in its highest form into the acres we want to control.

Olmsted replied:

> I can't tell you, I say again, how attractive to me the essential business we had together is; nor how I abhor the squabbles with the Commission and the politicians. Both are very deep with me—I feel them deeper every year. It was a passion thwarted and my whole life is really embittered with it very much and I think a good deal how I should like to show you what I really am and could do with a perfectly free and fair understanding from the start, and with moderate degree of freedom from the necessity of accommodating myself to infernal scoundrels. I have a perfect craving for the park, sometimes, and for an exposition from you of what I want.
>   But bother!
> Your plans are excellent, of course, you don't play with it but go at once to the essential starting points, and I hope

the Commissioners are wise enough to comprehend it. I think the ground looks attractive, as if you could form a much simpler and grander and more convenient kind of park than any on it.

Olmsted's health was still precarious. Even though his association with the ill-fated Mariposa Mines was drawing to a close, he thought he would stay on in California to nurture other investments that would leave his family well provided for, should he die.

Vaux continued to urge him to return to New York.

> There is a nauseous sort of flavor about Park matters to me that it will be difficult to get over this side of the grave. However, never say die. . . . We may have some fun together yet. I wish you could have seen your destiny in our art. God meant you should. I really believe at times, although he may have something different for you to do, yet he cannot have anything nobler in store for you.

Olmsted was reluctant to confuse avocation with aptitude. Curiously, he still considered himself a dabbler in landscape art:

> I am sorry to say that I do not feel myself capable of being a landscape gardener, properly speaking, but I have a better and more cultivated taste in that department of art than any other, very much—having none in any other—and if I had the necessary quality of memory, or if my memory had been educated in botany and gardening when I was young, I might have been. But I can do anything with proper assistants, or money enough—anything that any man can do. I can combine means to ends better than most, and I love beautiful landscapes and rural recreations and people in rural recrea-

tions—better than anybody else I know. But I don't feel strong on the art side. I don't feel myself an artist, I feel rather as if it was sacrilegious in me to post myself in the portals of art. . . .

I have none of your feeling of nauseousness about the park. There is no other place in the world that is as much home to me. I love it all through and all the more for the trials it has cost me.

I should like my will to go into the Brooklyn Park, or anything else—if I really believed I could get a decent living out of it—but in landscape work in general I never had any ground for supposing that I could. You used to argue that I might hope to—that's all. I could never see it.

Fortunately, Olmsted's despairing assessment of his future as a landscape designer did not govern his actions, and in November, 1865, he found himself back in New York to plunge once again into his difficult love affair with Central Park and to begin working out with Vaux the details of the design of Prospect Park. Thus, it was thanks to Calvert Vaux that the restless and mercurial Olmsted was propelled—this time once and for all—into his life's career.

Facilitating the design of Prospect Park was the boundary revision that eliminated Flatbush Avenue and provided a better-shaped site with which the landscape architects could work than the long, narrow rectangle of Central Park had been. The topographical configuration was also favorable to the designers, as the park is situated on the terminal moraine deposited in the wake of the last period of North American glaciation, and this gives it its gently undulating character.

Adhering to Vaux's original tripartite scheme of meadow, woods and water, the collaborators arranged their views and vistas of sylvan scenery (Ill. 92). Conceiving recreation to be primarily a visual experience, they laid out pathways and carriage ways as a series of vantage points for enjoying the park's carefully arranged landscape compositions. The Long Meadow was artfully designed as an antidote to the surrounding city where one's vision was forever checked by walls or channeled down the straight lines of grid thoroughfares. Little hillocks fringed by woods tease the eye, fostering the illusion that beyond the last rise there is no busy city, no buildings, no traffic, only boundless horizon.

In the Long Meadow, the dominant theme of pastoral scenery was struck, the central motif in the design of Prospect Park. In the report accompanying their plan, Olmsted and Vaux were quite specific about what constituted pastoral scenery. "It consists of combinations of trees, standing singly or in groups, and casting their shadows over broad stretches of turf, or repeating their beauty by reflection upon the calm surface of pools. . . ." Incidental effects to enliven and give variety to the whole, though subordinate, could be incorporated into the basic pastoral scheme: "rugged ravines shaded with trees, and made picturesque with shrubs," as well as "some slight approach to the mystery, variety and luxuriance of tropical scenery . . . gay with flowers, and intricate and mazy with vines and creepers, ferns, rushes and broad-leaved plants."

The forest groves between the Long Meadow and the Nether-mead are the picturesque counterpart of the Central Park Ramble. A little stream, with a series of pools created by water pumped from the lake, meanders like a mountain brook through these woods. On an island in the lake, Olmsted chose cold-tolerant plants whose forms simulated the tropical vegetation he had admired so much in Panama.

He and Vaux realized, however, that people visit parks not only to admire nature but to socialize with one another. They observed, "Men must come together, and must be seen coming together, in carriages, on horseback and on foot, and the concourse of animated life which will thus be formed, must in itself be made, if possible, an attractive and diverting spectacle." It was clear that if the impression of tranquillity and rural seclusion was to be maintained in certain parts of the park, there must be other places specifically set aside for congregation and social intercourse. Again, Central Park furnished the designers with some basic assumptions regarding public taste. Taking the circuit of the park's drives in one's landau or brougham had become an established social rite with people of fashion. Concerts in the park were another extremely popular amusement enjoyed by people of all classes. Skillfully, the designers made provisions combining both of these pleasures in Prospect Park. A music stand romantically sited on an island in the bay of the lake faced a pedestrian concourse, with shaded seats accommodating as many as ten thousand people, and this was flanked by two carriage concourses.

Another oval carriage concourse was provided on Vanderbilt Hill for visitors to the Lookout, a viewing tower that was never built, although the unadorned hillcrest is still a cool and pleasant eminence for a bird's-eye view of the park and its now-urbanized environs. Another planned but never-realized gathering place was the Refectory, designed like a country inn and sited on the lake shore where it could serve skaters in winter and boating parties in summer. In this way Prospect Park was planned to satisfy two antithetical needs—the need for tranquillity and solitude and the need for animated spectacle and gregariousness.

The 1866 report to the Brooklyn park commissioners extended its purview beyond the boundaries of Prospect Park and showed evidence of Olmsted's growing concern with matters of urban planning. Already recognizing the demand to use Central Park as a repository for various institutional structures, Olmsted and Vaux wished to obviate similar encroachments in Prospect Park. They suggested that part of the land east of Flatbush Avenue, which had been previously acquired but which they had recommended discarding for park purposes, be reserved for museums and other educational edifices. Suggestions were made for the remapping of some of the streets facing the principal entrance in order that, when developed, they might intersect its double-crescent plaza at a better angle. Other entrances were to be dignified by the creation of circles opening onto them.

Much more important than these minor rearrangements in the street pattern adjacent to the park was the proposal labeled "suburban connections." Though the word "park way" would not be coined until Olmsted and Vaux submitted their report of 1868, the concept was embodied in the 1866 report. "Such a road," they stated, "whatever may be the character of the country through which it passes, should be in itself of a picturesque character. It should, therefore, be neither very straight nor very level, and should be bordered by a small belt of trees and shrubbery." Specifically, Olmsted and Vaux had in mind a pleasure drive connecting the park with the sea. Ocean Parkway, when built, was straight, not curvilinear, but its functional separation of traffic by tree-planted malls into carriage way, walks, and access roads is an important innovation in the history of American road building.

If a single road for pleasure driving was good, even better would be an entire system of scenic roads. Anticipating the Queensboro Bridge, Olmsted and Vaux envisioned another parkway starting from Prospect Park and carried over the East River at Welfare Island to connect with Central Park. They hoped that north of Central Park the future development of Manhattan could incorporate an additional system of scenic roads to take the pleasure driver within sight of the Hudson and the Palisades.

Following its submission, the plan for Prospect Park was circulated among the citizens of Brooklyn. With far less division of opinion than had been the case with Central Park, it was

Music Island, Prospect Park, c. 1885.

declared acceptable, and an application to the state legislature to authorize the proposed boundary change was made. On May 29, 1866, Olmsted and Vaux were formally appointed landscape architects for the park. Cart gangs and barrow gangs were hired, and the labor of grading, filling, and draining was begun. Fourteen thousand trees were set out as initial stock in two nurseries on the park premises.

In their report of the following year, the landscape architects articulated once again the parkway concept. This time they proposed laying out such a road in anticipation of the development that would take place to the east of Prospect Park. They held that a spacious and agreeable thoroughfare would attract the settlement of families desiring suburban villas. When built, Eastern Parkway, like Ocean Parkway, was straight in the manner of a French boulevard, rather than picturesque with "frequent curves and considerable inequalities of surface" as Olmsted and Vaux

had suggested. Its real importance was as a demonstration of the relationship between transportation and urban development, an idea Olmsted and Vaux expounded at considerable length in their 1868 report to the Brooklyn park commissioners.

A landmark document in the history of city planning, this report is a brief for the differentiation of various classes of roads according to their intended function and adjacent land use. It included a review of the nature and condition of roads from feudal times to the nineteenth century, from the random footpaths of the medieval town to the grid plan of the urban land speculator. It pointed out how London merchants, ignoring Christopher Wren's sensible street widening and straightening proposal following the Great Fire, rebuilt their town on old property lines rather than in a logical form that would serve the common interest. The result was the delay for a century of a pattern of straight, connected streets with raised sidewalks for pedestrians and gutters underlain by sewers for carrying away refuse.

According to the authors of the 1868 report, now that cities were no longer compact defense fortresses with houses and workshops occupying the same structures, the whole urban mass tightly packed behind walls, a great amelioration of the human condition had occurred. There was a lower rate of disease and pestilence, fewer fires, and less vandalism and mob violence. Clairvoyantly, Olmsted and Vaux predicted the phenomenal urban growth of the twentieth century; they foresaw the spread of the city over a larger and larger land base. Devoted as they were to the aesthetic of the pastoral, they nevertheless saw the futility of trying to turn the clock back to an earlier, simpler America. They grasped the implications of the new technology that was being developed in the years immediately after the Civil War: the laying of the transatlantic cable, the construction of the railroad to the Pacific, the opening of the Orient to steam navigation. These and other innovations in transportation and communications would, they predicted, greatly stimulate trade, thereby making the enlargement of cities inevitable. The same technology that brought people together in cities also made it possible for them to spread out and live in relative seclusion from one another. The suburb with its leafy gardens was the product of the commuter railroad and the macadam highway.

The suburban ideal, discredited in our own time because its realization has so frequently been undistinguished in terms of design, was an important nineteenth-century contribution to the art of city building. Olmsted's work as a sanitarian during the war had given him firsthand exposure to the evils of crowded living conditions. The suburb promised pure air and sunlight and the oxygen-generating capacity of green plants surrounding each domicile. He firmly believed that the detached villa was a far healthier residence than the row house, the basic middle-class dwelling type of that day, and he never ceased campaigning for the subdivision of land into lots one hundred or more feet in width. The suburb, like the park, served a psychophysical purpose. It was a good compromise in the instinctive quest for verdure, which most people, particularly those who had once lived in the country, felt in the engulfing city. Its gardenesque attributes were a tonic for tired nerves.

Olmsted and Vaux believed that while a grid street plan was advantageous in the commercial sector, where the direct movement of goods was a desideratum, it was incompatible with a residential neighborhood. The widespread use of the new lightweight carriages dictated the need for smooth roadbeds, and the popularity of driving as a form of recreation dictated the need for pleasant, tree-shaded thoroughfares, preferably curvilinear, connecting parks with the residential quarter. To prohibit commercial traffic on such roads would be impossible, as the homes adjoining them would have to be serviced by vehicles of trade. Thus, the Prospect Park designers offered the parkway with its central drive, flanking promenades, exterior access roads and sidewalks, all separated by rows of trees, as a logical refinement in the history of road building to meet the needs of the nineteenth-century city. In addition, they reasoned the width of this multipurpose thoroughfare made it a perfect fire barrier.

The parkway system emanating from Prospect Park was the frame upon which residential Brooklyn would grow. Stranahan and his colleagues on the park commission wanted to ensure that Brooklyn would become more than a bedroom community of clerks and stenographers. By primarily catering to those who could afford to own carriages and build villas, Olmsted and Vaux can be criticized as elitists. (To their disappointment, row houses were built on the land bordering Ocean and Eastern parkways instead of the detached villas they had recommended.) But by extending the range of their concern from their immediate commission, the design of Prospect Park, to the entire undeveloped section of Brooklyn, they articulated the importance of intelligent, comprehensive planning in advance of future growth at a time when that kind of foresight was practically unknown.

The New York That Might Have Been

[New York] has come at last, far up on the West side, into possession of her birthright, into the roused consciousness that some possibility of a river-front may still remain to her; though, obviously, a justified pride in this property has yet to await the birth of a more responsible sense of style in her dealings with it, the dawn of some adequate plan or controlling idea.

Henry James, *The American Scene*

One wonders if a field embracing as many collective disciplines as city planning is a true profession. Certainly the term "city planner" is an inflated one, implying as it does an individual empowered to create the physical and social mold that will contain and shape thousands of human lives. In reality, for better or worse, the ultimate decisions concerning how cities get built are made by politicians, community sentiment, and the market mechanism. Ancillary to these is the planning fraternity, composed of engineers, social scientists, economists, architects, and landscape architects.

It is not surprising, then, that Olmsted had trouble defining what he considered his profession to be. While he was still in California designing the community of Berkeley and the park system for San Francisco, he wrote to Vaux:

I am all the time bothered with the miserable nomenclature of L.A. *Landscape* is not a good word, *Architecture* is not; the combination is not—Gardening is worse. . . . The art is not gardening nor is it architecture. What I am doing here in California is neither. . . . The arrangement of village streets is neither *Landscape* Art, nor Architectural Art, nor is it both together in my mind, of course it is not, and it will never be in the popular mind. . . . If you are bound to establish this new art—you don't want an old name for it, and for clearness, for convenience, for distinctness, you do need half a dozen new technical words at least.

Lacking the imprecise label of city planner, he reluctantly accepted the title landscape architect and was known as such for the rest of his life, although his restless energies led him into practically all the allied provinces of planning: road building, mass transit, subdivision development, sanitary engineering. Prevented by the politics of his day, he was unable to deal with the ghetto in his philosophy of urbanism; central-city regeneration would have to await the crusading of a Jacob Riis and the housing reforms of the twentieth century. Still, Olmsted did deal with the slums at one remove by presenting parks as a palliative, an alternative to the gin house and a temporary escape from the congested misery of Chatham Square and Park Row.

His real genius lay in achieving a solid and workable marriage between city and country; the offspring of that union was the self-contained suburb. The suburb as Olmsted conceived it was not a suburb in the usual sense, but rather an entire planned community like an English garden city.

Olmsted recognized earlier than most the phenomenon of rural-urban migration that in the years following the Civil War was becoming the dominant social trend in American life, a trend that was to be a major theme of such writers as William Dean Howells, Theodore Dreiser, and Frank Norris. In *Public Parks and the Enlargement of Town*, a paper delivered to the American Social Science Association in 1870, he saw new channels of dependency being set up between town and country. More and more, the people of the country were relying on the city for merchandise and professional talent. Transportation dissolved distance, destroying local autonomy. Once-proud little New England villages were falling into decay as the country doctor, lawyer, schoolmaster, shoemaker, dressmaker, and storekeeper vanished from the scene. The symbol of a new life style was the railroad timetable that now hung beside the almanac in every farmhouse.

Olmsted did not deplore this trend. Rather, he rejoiced. Arguing against those who regarded the prevailing townward drift as a moral epidemic, he equated a return to ruralism with a return to feudalism, noting that "no nation has yet begun to give up schools or newspapers, railroads or telegraphs, to restore feudal rights or advance rates of postage. King-craft and priest-craft are nowhere gaining any solid ground." He felt that those forms of individual enterprise typical of the frontier had had their day and the time had come for a new corporate order. The same transportation technology that siphoned people off the farms and into the cities also created the daily commuter. No longer was it necessary to live in close proximity to one's place of business; the diurnal oscillation of the work force between the urban core and its outlying suburbs could now become a widespread way of life. In the 1868 report to the Brooklyn park commissioners, he

had drawn a portrait of an Horatio Alger type of young man likely to situate in the metropolis. He was a country boy whose acumen and ambition had outstripped the opportunities of the provincial town near the place of his birth and who, "being of superior calibre, ultimately finds himself drawn by irresistible magnetic force to the commercial cities." There he succeeds and becomes wealthy. But for this individual, riches alone do not suffice; atavistically he longs for nature. "Trees and grass are, however, wrought into the very texture and fibre of his constitution and without being aware of it he feels day by day that his life needs a suggestion of the old country flavor to make it palatable as well as profitable"—in other words, the suburb.

Olmsted noticed the attraction the town held for women especially. Prefiguring Dreiser's *Sister Carrie,* he analyzed the urge that propelled them into the new American cities as "a frantic desire to escape from the dull lives which they have seen before them in the country, a craving for recreation, especially for more companionship in yielding to playful girlish impulses, innocent in themselves." Nor was the townward migration of females a frivolous thing. The civilized woman wanted neatness in her surroundings and labor-saving conveniences in her daily life. Concentration of population made possible the provision of goods and services impossible in the country. It allowed for a standard of municipal housekeeping—clean streets, sewers, garbage removal—that appealed to a woman's instinct for tidiness and order. Olmsted pointed out that extreme density was not necessary to enjoy these fruits of modern technology:

Probably the advantages of civilization can be found illustrated and demonstrated under no other circumstances as in some suburban neighborhoods where each family abode stands fifty or a hundred feet or more apart from all others, and at some distance from the public road. And it must be remembered, also, that man's enjoyment of rural beauty has clearly increased rather than diminished with his advance in civilization. There is no reason, except in the loss of time, the inconvenience, discomfort, and expense of our present arrangements for short travel, why suburban advantages should not be almost indefinitely extended.

While Olmsted deplored the polluted air, the dirt, the congestion, the noise of the central city (noise particularly jangled his sensitive nerves so that he often had to work at night after the din of metal cart wheels and horses' hooves clattering on paving stones had died down), he valued the cultural opportunities of the metropolis and predicted with equanimity "larger towns than any the world has yet known." Cities were the places where one was educated, edified, entertained. He believed "the further progress of civilization is to depend mainly upon the influences by which men's minds and characters will be affected while living in large towns."

He conceded, however, that simply to extend the city in its present form would be to preserve the pathologies of the past. The villain was density. His prescription was to house as large a percentage of the population as possible in detached single-family dwellings; then there would be a corresponding reduction of crime and disease. For the anomie of the crowd he would substitute the neighborliness of the community.

Much of Olmsted's ideal city of the future was embodied in the plan for Brooklyn, a plan he would elaborate in Boston and Buffalo. Just as the green or common was the center of the old New England village, the park would be the heart of the town. It should therefore be planned in conjunction with the arteries of circulation of the rest of the system, "trunk routes of communication between it and the distant parts of the town existing or forecasted." These routes should preferably be "narrow informal elongations of the park," picturesquely harmonizing with topography; if that was impossible because of a prearranged street plan, straight formal parkways in the manner of the boulevards of Paris, which he had studied and admired, would suffice. Olmsted said. "It is a common error to regard a park as something to be produced complete in itself, as a picture painted on canvas. It should rather be planned as one to be done in fresco, with constant consideration of exterior objects, some of them quite at a distance and even existing as yet only in the imagination of the painter."

In changing his focus from the park to the town, Olmsted changed the optical properties of the metaphorical Claude glass, the device through which picturesque critics viewed nature as a series of self-contained vignettes. When carriage travel over smoothly graded parkways became a popular pastime, "picturesqueness" became something kinetic. Translating this into modern terms, one can say that to the extent that scenic appreciation is a motive for automobile travel today, its optical symbol is the movie, not the still, camera.

Olmsted's basic blueprint of parkways radiating out from a park and connecting it with the residential sector and perhaps with other parks as well was grounded in a concept of social benefit. Such a planning framework would produce a healthier, more domestic environment. Always, however, whenever this abstract ideal was made specific in the various commissions he carried out first with Vaux and later with other assistants, close attention was given to aesthetic considerations. Indeed, Olmsted could never divorce social and aesthetic goals; beauty, especially the beauty of trees and grass and water, was for him an ameliorating and therapeutic force. Moreover, it was a sound investment. Just as he had in his books on the South argued the case against slavery on economic grounds, so, too, he was at pains to point out the economic wisdom inherent in a well-designed road and recreation system. Handsome tree-lined parkways and land-

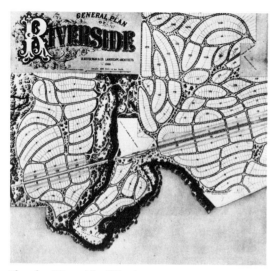

Plan for Riverside, Illinois, 1869.

scaped parks would attract fine dwellings and maintain high land values on their borders and in their adjacent precincts.

In 1868 he and Vaux had their first opportunity to design a complete suburban community, Riverside, on the Des Plaines River outside Chicago. It stands today as one of the few realized community-development plans that they produced, an example of what portions of New York might have become had their subsequent designs for Staten Island, northern Manhattan, and the Bronx been carried out.

First, they proposed a six-mile parkway connecting the suburb with the city. Although Riverside was served by commuter railroad, how much pleasanter, they reasoned, for a businessman to combine exercise and recreation with the journey to work by riding in a carriage or on horseback over a well-designed parkway. On holidays, people from the city could use the parkway to come for "rural fêtes" at Riverside.

Owing to the resistance of landowners along the proposed right-of-way, the parkway was the one component of the Riverside scheme that was never built. Nothing perhaps separates our own age more from Olmsted's than the concept of travel it embodies. The bridle path beside the parkway was to be arranged so that "equestrians at pleasure turn from it to converse with friends in carriages." Clearly, sociability and the enjoyment of scenery belong to the leisurely pace of the parkway, whereas the modern expressway serves the traveler whose only object is his destination.

The plan of Riverside is in appearance organic, cellular. It was certainly a radical departure from the typical land speculator's grid layout. The designers recommended a road pattern of "gracefully curved lines, generous spaces, and the absence of sharp corners, the idea being to suggest and imply leisure, contemplativeness and happy tranquility." In the interstices of the irregularly shaped blocks thus formed are open spaces of the "character of informal village greens, commons and playgrounds." Massive street tree planting along picturesque principles, plus the stipulation that each individual homeowner must maintain at least two trees between his house and the road, was insurance against the obtrusiveness of possible architectural eyesores.

An aerial view of New York City today shows, except for Riverside Drive, which was designed by Olmsted, and a few residential enclaves such as Riverdale in the Bronx or Forest Hills Gardens in Queens (the latter, incidentally, was laid out by Frederick Law Olmsted, Jr., in the early years of the twentieth century), a relentless geometry, an endless repetition and multiplication of uniform rectangular blocks and straight streets. It is hard to believe that this ubiquitous urban mass covering 320 square miles was, less than a hundred years ago, largely farms, that there were high ridges of exposed bedrock, untenanted woods, streams, ponds, and marshes. Such was the *tabula rasa* of the nineteenth-century planner. Such was the opportunity presented Olmsted, the opportunity of planning new communities in a fresh, unspoiled setting. Unfortunately, his plans for New York were aborted. Now the marshes have been filled, ponds drained, streams buried underground, woods chopped, bedrock blasted away, and the opportunity of utilizing nature as a partner in the design process has, except in a few remote corners of the city, disappeared forever.

The latest city land to be parceled out according to the convenient and unaesthetic grid is on Staten Island, New York's fastest growing borough since the opening of the Verrazano Bridge in 1964. Staten Island's transfer from rural to urban status was retarded by its pre-bridge insularity and, in Olmsted's day, by the notoriety it enjoyed as an unhealthy environment. Malaria was the specter scaring away would-be settlers. This had not been true during the years of his residence on the island as a young gentleman farmer; then such notables as Judge William Emerson, brother of the Concord philosopher, had lived there. Theodore Roosevelt's family had kept a summer home near Fresh Kills until after the Civil War. But by 1870 the island had passed out of fashion as a place of residence and a place of resort, and Olmsted was called in to head up a team of consultants including the pioneer sanitarian Dr. Elisha Harris and the architect Henry Hobson Richardson to investigate the causes for the island's decline and suggest remedies that would make it attractive to settlement once again.

In his report, Olmsted traced the decline of Staten Island from a pleasant agricultural community when "the owners of the land lived in quaint and cozy, low-roofed and broad-galleried cottages, approached by the most delightful class of summer roads, winding among the great trees, crossing clear brooks and skirting the smooth, clean meadows," to its present decrepitude. The cutting of forests and the abandonment of farms to idle land speculation had caused the ground to lose its porosity and led to the formation of over a thousand pools—pernicious malarial nurseries.

Science had not yet isolated the mosquito as the carrier of malaria. Dr. John Strong Newberry, geologist and physician and another consultant on the study team, thought the disease might be caused by "a granular microphyte" or "by certain gases or volatile emanations . . . evoked by decaying vegetable matter under the required conditions of temperature and moisture." Shade trees, their canopies of foliage warding off heat and their roots draining the soil, were seen as a foil to the steamy, stagnant ponds dotting the island. To entirely eradicate the scourge, however, thorough underdrainage of its particularly water-retentive soil was considered necessary.

When Olmsted was a Staten Island farmer, he had been especially interested in techniques of drainage; indeed, he had rationalized leaving his farm for his extended tour of England on the grounds of studying modern drainage methods there. He had made extensive use of drainage tiles in Central and Prospect parks. Now he recommended a network of open-jointed pipes leading from all the soggy places and from individual properties on the island into public drains connected to outfalls on its perimeter. Only in this way, he argued, could Staten Island be made wholesome and fit for habitation. Shade trees bordering a comprehensive system of "high-roads" would further alleviate the problem and be a picturesque inducement to a better class of settlement. Unfortunately, the plan depicting these roads has been lost, and their outlines can only be reconstructed from the description in the report.

One must also rely on the written word to visualize the system of impounding reservoirs Olmsted and his colleagues proposed for the eastern half of the island. While the watershed surrounding three "dales" where collection basins would be formed could be used for park purposes (Fairmount Park in Philadelphia was a precedent for this kind of combined land use), Olmsted doubted the practicality of such an undertaking on Staten Island. Rather, he proposed what he called the Water Glade, open meadows bordering the water-courses and impounding reservoirs. The Water Glade would be rimmed by highways, and beyond them would be the Overdale, land restricted against any nuisance occupations damaging to the adjacent water supply, although private dwellings with certain safeguards could be built upon it.

Nowhere on the island did Olmsted think it suitable to build other than detached houses. The minimum lot size where land was more in demand near the shore should be one-quarter acre; five acres in the upland areas he estimated to be the maximum for a suburban residence.

In domestic arrangements, he wished to break open the stuffy Victorian box; every house he felt should have "a series of out-of-door apartments, not open to the public view, in which direct exposure to sun and wind may, when desired, be avoided, and in which various ordinary household occupations may be carried on."

He maintained that, "With good, shaded highways, walks not liable to be overthronged, it is not at all necessary that the house should command fine, distant or general views, it is rather better that stand-points for these should be possessed by each family in common with others, at some little distance from the house, so as to afford inducement and occasion for going more out from it, and for realizing and keeping up acquaintances by the eye at least, with the community." Thus, as in his park plans. Olmsted's ideal suburb accommodated the need for both privacy and sociability.

The Staten Island report was never acted upon, but some of the ideas it embodied were carried out later in other Olmsted projects, notably the use of drainage basins for flood control and to preserve a green chain of open spaces within the urban mass. The Boston Back Bay with its surrounding Fenway is one example.

In 1876 Olmsted had an opportunity to further elaborate his theories of residential planning when he was commissioned with J. James R. Croes, a civil and topographical engineer, to produce a

plan for the twenty-third and twenty-fourth wards of New York City (northern Manhattan and land recently annexed from Westchester County in what is now the Bronx). The topography Olmsted and Croes were hired to study is composed of long northeast-trending ridges of Fordham gneiss, the bedrock of the Bronx, and a high escarpment of Manhattan schist. This corrugated land was ideal for picturesque treatment. Nowhere in his writings does Olmsted attack the prevailing grid method of laying out streets so systematically and persuasively as in this report. The defects he pointed out are, by and large, with us today.

First, there was the mindless uniformity of blocks sixty-six yards wide by two hundred yards long, which meant that "if a building site is wanted, whether with a view to a church or a blast furnace, an opera house or a toy shop, there is, of intention, no better a place in one of these blocks than in another." Furthermore, the artificial boundaries of these blocks imposed rigid constraints on the size and shape of the buildings that occupied them. Cathedral, convent, university, factory, depot—none could extend more than sixty-six yards from north to south. Conversely, no museum, library, post office, or hotel could, unless it were two hundred feet wide, be lighted by windows and entered on both its east and west sides.

Olmsted pointed out yet another aesthetic disadvantage: "There is no place under the system in New York where a stately building can be looked up to from base to turret, none where it can even be seen full in the face and all at once taken in by the eye; none where it can be viewed in advantageous perspective."

Worse than any of these limitations, however, were the implications of the street system on housing, particularly in that pre-reform age when tenements were fetid warrens with sunless, airless interior rooms. The uniform block size meant a standard lot depth of one hundred feet, a lot too large to be afforded by the clerk or mechanic and too small for the wealthy merchant. The

Manhattan street plan, 1872.

nonexistence of alleys meant, as it does today, that all service deliveries had to be made and all garbage collected from the front sidewalk. High ground rents forced the division of blocks into more numerous and therefore more narrow house lots; to gain the same amount of square footage as on a wider lot, houses were extended to the maximum depth possible. The results were rooms badly proportioned, poorly ventilated, and dependent on distant skylights for natural illumination.

Such were the general defects of the uniform street grid in residential areas. Worse yet was its application to rugged terrain, such as that of northern Manhattan and the Bronx, where steep grades would necessitate the employment of two horses, whereas one would suffice if the streets wound around the hillsides. There were other diseconomies inherent in a plan of formal, straight streets. To be attractive, a straight street must be laid out with particular care with "as perfect lines and as perfect surfaces in its curbs, gutters and lamp-posts, pavement and flagging, as the densely occupied street of the city." Trees must be spaced beside it with exact regularity, and the street and its related landscape features maintained with great particularity. On the contrary, a certain unkemptness was the very essence of picturesque roads:

Wild plants may spring up, here and there, in random tufts, or, again, the roadsides be all filled out (as some in the district now are), with a thick growth of low brambles, ferns, aster, gentians, golden-rods; roadside trees may be irregularly spaced and of various sizes and species, great opposite small, asp over against maple, elm bending to oak; fine old trees may be left standing, and, to save them, the wheel-way carried a little to the right or left, or slightly raised or lowered. It may be desirable, simply for convenience sake, to go to the expense of avoiding such conditions, but, as a matter of taste, they are far from blemishes; they add to other charms of picturesqueness, and they are a concession to nature, tending to an effect not of incongruity and incompleteness, but of consistent and happy landscape composition.

Already in 1876 it was not enough to design with nature; one must also design with technology. All the miles of wires and pipes and tracks we take so much for granted today, so that they, not topography, seem to us the real substructure of the city, were then just about to be laid in place. We complain that we live in an antiquated urban machine as we cope with a deteriorating transportation system, streets with potholes and cracked pavements, garbage-strewn sidewalks. Optimistically, Olmsted's generation invested in the first mechanical improvements that were designed to make life more efficient, convenient, and pleasant. As Olmsted put it, "Before New York can have doubled its present population, new motive powers and means of transit, new methods of building, new professions and trades, and new departures in sanitary science, if not in political science, are likely to have appeared."

Anticipating the demand for mass transit, the plan for the twenty-third and twenty-fourth wards contained a proposal for a steam railroad system, separate from the existing through railroads and designed specifically for the daily commuter. Extending the principle of grade separation of traffic he had first utilized in the Central Park circulation system, Olmsted pointed out that by utilizing topography, "intersecting streets may be carried over or under it, as local convenience may dictate, with moderate expense." He recommended a system of loop lines that would pro-

vide communication between the east and west sections of the Bronx, as well as more frequent service to the central city, with the same number of trains.

It is clear, then, that the picturesque suburb was not a sentimental rural conceit grafted on to a modern world, a planner's version of Marie Antoinette playing milkmaid. Olmsted faced one of the most pervasive dichotomies of American civilization—the persistence of the pastoral ideal in an increasingly technological society. He was convinced that the machinery of the new urbanism could be accommodated within a framework where nature and human beings remained dominant. Indeed, it was machine technology as embodied in the steam train, telegraph, asphalt paving, and lightweight delivery wagon that made the picturesque suburb possible at all. Unfortunately, commercial, not social, motives have tended to rule our society, and technology has been allowed to pollute rather than improve the environment and diminish the quality of life not only in the cities but in the suburbs.

Small Parks

One of the unfortunate side effects of Central Park was that, with the construction of one major pleasure ground, the practice of laying out Manhattan around a series of residential squares was more or less abandoned. Though Downing had castigated them as "mere paddocks," Stuyvesant, Madison, and Union squares, Gramercy and St. John's parks were pleasant oases of green in the gray urban grid. After the 1850's, the development of mass transportation—first horse-drawn, later elevated steam railroads—meant that large numbers of people could collect in Central Park rather than distributing themselves into a variety of local grounds. At the same time, the escalation of real estate values made the reservation of land from the development process increasingly expensive. More and more, the only land to be bypassed in the onrushing tide of urbanization was that which was topographically unsuitable for building: swamps and excessively steep slopes. It was often these rejected scraps of land, conveniently labeled parks, that Olmsted was given to design.

He, of course, would have preferred a less commercial and more social basis for the selection and siting of parks. In a speech of 1870, "Parks and the Enlargement of Towns," Olmsted had commented in passing on the desirability of having "small grounds so distributed through a large town that some one of them could be easily reached by a short walk from every house." He envisioned that these would be laid out in conjunction with a system of parkways, forming a green chain in the residential sector of the city.

Olmsted had another reason for recommending a series of small parks: to prevent encroachments upon his large-scale parks where the primary motive was landscape composition. He could hardly have anticipated the extent to which the concept of recreation would be transformed from an aesthetic pastime to a physical activity in the twentieth century. He would be shocked to see how Central Park has been parceled into baseball diamonds, soccer fields, tennis courts, bowling greens, croquet lawns, and playgrounds. Perhaps, had Olmsted's intentions been honored and numerous neighborhood parks and playing fields been built, more of Central Park's original scenic character might have been preserved.

In Brooklyn in the 1870's, Olmsted and Vaux were given the opportunity to design two small parks, Fort Greene (also known as Washington Park) and Tompkins Park. Fort Greene, on the Brooklyn Heights with a commanding view of New York harbor, had been hastily built during the War of 1812. The site of the demolished fort had been set aside as a park, partly for its historical association and partly for its eminence, which made it impractical to develop. A tomb containing the remains of some of the 11,000 patriots who had perished because of barbarous treatment on British prison ships during the Revolution was to be incorporated in the design. The park was also to contain a meeting ground where large assemblages could gather to hear political oratory, an important function of parks in the pre-television era.

In addition to its public function, Fort Greene was to have

its domestic side, serving the neighborhood around it. In keeping with Olmsted's notion that formality suited the "gregarious" parts of a park and informality and rusticity the "neighborly" zones, the designers arranged the public meeting ground, prison martyrs' monument, and a hilltop area for military exercises axially; the rest of the park was laid out in curvilinear walks bordered by massed trees encircling open, grassy spaces. The basic lines of this scheme are still intact; however, the public meeting ground is now a children's playground and a column commemorating the prison martyrs, an addition to the original design that only included the crypt, is done in a neoclassical manner that is foreign to the Olmsted-Vaux style.

Tompkins Park is only one-fourth the size of Fort Greene Park, and there the designers did not have as complicated a program to fit into the site. It was clearly too small to attempt even a minimum of natural landscape effects, as at Fort Greene. To create a bright and cheerful residential square, the designers decided to abandon their usual formula of an exterior tree-shaded mall around the park's periphery in favor of turf and flowering shrubs. Ordinarily in an Olmsted and Vaux design, one would glimpse patches of sunlit meadow in the park proper through the foliage of these exterior malls. In this little park, it would be the trees that would occupy the central territory—not trees irregularly massed, but a formal plantation surrounded at first by turf but later, when the park became more fully utilized, by gravel, as in the parks of France. This arrangement satisfied two clienteles of the park: the homeowners who looked out upon it had a cheerful and agreeable gardenlike view, and the general strolling public could be accommodated in its shady interior.

In 1873 Olmsted and Vaux were commissioned to design Morningside Park. As with many grounds they had to deal with over the years, Morningside was a remnant cut out of the urban fabric and discarded from the development process. It was not a swamp like the Boston Fenway or Jackson Park in Chicago; rather, it was a precipitous escarpment of Manhattan schist with a sheer rock face rising about one hundred feet above the Harlem plain. In a city single-mindedly dedicated to growing à la grid, this obstacle obviously could not be traversed. It presented, to say the least, an interesting problem in the art of landscape design.

After registering their initial complaint, the designers assessed the potential of the site for some kind of treatment that would not duplicate that offered by its neighbor, Central Park. The brow of the high escarpment was the vantage point for a fine view, now dimmed by air pollution and urban blight. Then, however, according to Olmsted and Vaux, you could gaze eastward "far out across a wide range of beautiful country, and over the waters and islands of the river and sound, the eastern sea-gate of the metropolis."

A series of balconies along the upper border of the park was proposed as viewing platforms giving out over this panorama. In the triangular basin formed between the declivity and the southeast corner of the park, the designers recommended an aquatic garden of subtropical plants. At 115th Street, where a break in the rock face occurs, they proposed a bold architectural feature, an esplanade and exhibition hall with staircases, steps, and walks leading down from the balconied terrace along Morningside Drive and up from Morningside Avenue. The grounds in this area of the park were to be treated in "an urban and gardenesque style" with fountains, flower beds, and statuary. North of this area, a walk carved into the base of the ledge was "to be deeply shaded and to have a wild, picturesque and secluded character." At 120th Street, it would open onto a quiet sunny lawn. The very craggy northwest panhandle of the park was to be an alpine rock garden.

This first plan for Morningside was shelved for fourteen years, years in which the burgeoning metropolis sprouted tentacles of railroad tracks into its former hinterland, and northern Manhattan became dotted with little groups of row houses. The area wore a raw frontier, half-baked air, with its unpaved streets and clusters of homes partially filling out one block here, another block someplace else.

When Olmsted and Vaux were recommissioned as designers of Morningside Park in 1887, they felt it necessary to revise their original plan. An elevated railroad had been built with a station at 116th Street, necessitating a new approach to the park and a walk connecting 116th Street on the east with 116th Street on the west. Rail service also meant the park should have the capacity to accommodate larger crowds than those from the immediate environs. The terrace bordering Morningside Drive with stairs descending into the park had been constructed along more imposing and formal lines than those envisioned by Olmsted and Vaux, but not in such a manner as to destroy the spirit of their original idea: "the aggrandizing of the view downward and eastward from the west side, and the freshening, gracing and enriching of the view upward and westward from the east side."

Paralleling the terraced mall with its eastward-facing balconies they recommended a walk along the base of the ledge. Here, instead of a sweeping vista, the visitor would be offered "a sense of retirement and seclusion, and of immediately surrounding sylvan quietude." The suggested planting for the cliff-face beside this walk was thoroughly romantic in character. In its thin pockets of soil, a profusion of vines and creepers were to be densely planted, which, when seen from the walkway below, would appear "fold upon fold of them mingling with projections of the gray ledge." The plan also called for a rambling ground and "Restawhile" pavilion on the plateau and a brightly lighted path across the park at 116th Street.

In 1875 Olmsted was asked to advise the Department of Public Parks on the laying out of Riverside Drive and Riverside Park. He insisted that the two be treated integrally, that the imaginary line dividing them be erased. In 1868 the first segment of Riverside Avenue, as it was then called, had been built, a sharply curving thoroughfare with many abrupt changes of grade. With his usual consideration for existing topography, Olmsted replanned its course as a serpentine thoroughfare maintaining gently undulating grades. Instead of massing trees within the long, narrow park strip where they would block the fine view of the Hudson River, he recommended they be planted among the lanes of the drive.

Olmsted proved that the small park could take many forms and serve a variety of functions. In Riverside it was long and linear, an adjunct to the drive; Morningside provided a scenic promenade and romantic rambling ground; Tompkins Park was a cheerful and refreshing square; Fort Greene was a place for public meetings and military demonstrations. Now, a hundred years after they were built, these parks exist, much mutilated and poorly maintained, but still testifying to Olmsted and Vaux's artistry.

Conclusion

To see New York's parks today is to realize the extent to which Olmsted's *rus in urbe* ideal has been distorted. The rambling ground in Morningside Park is now a weed-choked waste, and the alpine garden has been blanketed over by a school. Only a vestige of Tompkins Park in Brooklyn remains; its central plantation of trees has been replaced by a community center. Music Island in the lake in Prospect Park, where bands used to play on summer evenings, has disappeared beneath a popular but ugly skating rink.

Central Park, like an overdecorated Christmas tree, has more than its share of tinsel excrescences. It has its lakeside skating rinks, a Walt Disney–style kiddie barnyard, metal swings and slides, and other paraphernalia of play. Where sheep once grazed on gleaming grass are baseball diamonds of bald dirt. Parking lots have put a pall of gray asphalt over other once-green portions of the park.

The erosion of the Olmsted-Vaux heritage over the years has been caused by a variety of forces: the general acceptance of a new standard of beauty, primarily architectural in nature, after the Columbian Exposition of 1893; the growing popularity of sports and the increasingly physical character of recreation; the vulnerability of parks to encroachments by donors of memorial gifts and by public agencies and institutions wishing to expand their facilities; and the increasing debasement of maintenance standards and the attrition of maintenance personnel.

Even in Olmsted's lifetime these forces were at work. As early as 1866 Richard Morris Hunt designed a series of gates for the entrances to Central Park. Like Hunt's 1902 design for the Metropolitan Museum, whose neoclassical halls eclipsed Vaux's original modest Victorian structure, the gates were entirely foreign to the spirit of rurality in the park. Olmsted and Vaux successfully fended off these unnecessary elaborations of their original scheme.

A generation later, however, the proponents of urban architectural grandeur, bolstered by the public appetite for neoclassicism that had been whetted by the "White City" that had risen on the shores of Lake Michigan in 1893, triumphed in Prospect Park. This time their standard bearer was Stanford White, whose firm of McKim, Mead and White was commissioned to prepare a plan for embellishing the entrances to the park. Olmsted had tactfully compromised his own artistic principles to achieve a stylistic harmony with the Beaux Arts motive of the Columbian Exposition. Now, appalled that the ruling motive of Prospect Park—rural scenery—could so completely be set aside, and aware that a battle of styles was at hand, he wrote to a friend in 1895:

> Now I want you to take my assurance that there is a strenuous fight coming on between those of our side and those who are disposed to revise every body of public land that has been laid out regardfully of natural beauty with the object of transforming it as far as possible into a field of architectural beauty. . . . Stanford White has been and is trying to estab-

lish the rule of motives that are at war with those that ruled in the original laying out of Brooklyn Park. He distinctly hates these older motives. He would at least, now that so much has been established in the spirit of the original design, make the Park an incongruous hybrid between that which was aimed at in this design and that which would be aimed at in such a design as a French architect would have made early in the century, introducing sentimental passages of "Nature," like that attempted at Petit Trianon, but making them secondary, and as interludes of efforts approaching the ruling Versailles character.

Olmsted stressed that it was not the architectural treatment of parks *per se* that he was against, but the incongruity of grafting grandiose architectural features on to a park whose primary aim was to provide relief from architecture.

What I am fighting is a *weak, fragmentary and vacillating compromise* between the two leading general motives. Such artificial elements as are necessary to convenience of public use in a park I believe in making, and sometimes I think it best to display and aggrandize the display of them. But I would make them distinctly as means for the better enjoyment of natural scenery where I well could.

As Henry Hope Reed and Sophia Duckworth have pointed out in their book *Central Park: A History and a Guide,* "equipment recreation," spurred by such reformers as Jacob Riis in New York and Jane Addams in Chicago, became an important feature of parks around the turn of the century. Twenty-seven playgrounds have now nibbled bites out of Central Park instead of being inserted into vest-pocket lots scattered through the surrounding community. The lower perimeter of Morningside Park is lined with a series of chain-link enclosures, recreational cages for the human animal.

Private philanthropy of dubious taste has studded the "Greensward" with bits of bronze. Olmsted and Vaux felt that statuary was an appropriate addition to the Mall; they would be displeased to see the host of heroic dead and fairy-tale favorites all over the southern half (the more publicly conspicuous half) of Central Park.

Even more destructive of the designers' intended rurality is the encroachment by buildings on their parks. In Prospect Park, while neoclassicism was in the saddle, in addition to the grandiose entrances, the Peristyle was added by McKim, Mead and White; and the Boathouse, Tennis House, and Willink Entrance Comfort Station by the firm of Helmle, Huberty and Hurdswell. Later constructions have further marred that park's original scenic composition without even having the distinction of being architecturally interesting. The encroachments upon Central Park have, with the exception of the Metropolitan Museum, been less monumental in scale than those in Prospect Park, but nevertheless a greater detraction. That Central Park has not long since succumbed and been completely built over or, as the current fashion would have it, built under (an underground parking garage, police stables, and fire communications center figure among recent proposals for the use of those valuable vacant acres) is due in large measure to the stewardship role of such self-appointed guardian groups as the Parks Council and the Friends of Central Park.

Perhaps the most lamentable aspect of New York's parks today is their degenerate maintenance. Olmsted once wrote a parable on this point.

A man may buy and fit up a costly house, but if, after he has done so, he finds coal and ashes scattered over his carpets, if decorated ceilings are stained and marred, if pictures are defaced, if books and dishes are piled on his chairs, windows and doors kept open during storms, beds used as tables and tables as beds, and so on, all that he has obtained for his expenditure will be of little value to him for the time being, and the possibility of its ever again being made of much value will lessen with every day that such misuse is suffered, through *inefficiency of housekeeping,* to prevail.

He would be shocked to know that, in spite of twentieth-century affluence, the City of New York can no longer afford to repair park benches and drinking fountains, mend broken pavements, plant grass, prevent lakes from silting up with debris.

It is, no doubt, foolishly sentimental to wish that anything so public as a park should, like a fine painting or sculpture, be held inviolate to change over a long period of time. It would be wrong to regard Central Park simply as a stage set, an artful arrangement of scenery for passive viewing; it is also a stage, an activity arena where people must be given an opportunity for self-expression. The twentieth-century concept of what constitutes recreation is necessarily different from the nineteenth. Certainly it is a more physical concept; we are a sports culture, and given the dearth of baseball diamonds, soccer fields, and tennis courts around the city, it is inevitable and probably right that people should use the park's lawns and meadows for these activities. Still, when one walks through the Ramble, that yet-green woodland haven of birds and other small forest creatures, one wishes that the rest of the park could be more like it once was. Here in the heart of the city, rugged, wild, picturesque, and more or less intact, is one passage of Olmsted and Vaux's "Greensward" symphony of rural scenery.

Parks should be places where people can gather and play, places where spontaneous, impromptu social experiences can occur. But parks must serve another need as well: even, or especially, in the machine age it is important in some way perhaps unmeasurable by the sciences of biology and psychology, but nonetheless real, for man to confirm with his senses that he lives in a world of seasonal rhythms—of vernal buds, falling leaves, drifting snow. Olmsted knew this. His parks are more than charming exercises in a quaint, outmoded style known as the picturesque. They are still, perhaps more than ever, a therapeutic, life-enhancing force, and for this reason they should be allowed to endure.

Illustrative Portfolio

William Alex

Frederick Law Olmsted: New York's First Master Planner

Over a thirty-five-year period of involvement with the city, Frederick Law Olmsted was the closest thing to a master planner New York ever had, from the design of Central Park in 1858 with Calvert Vaux, to the report on Columbia University's campus design with Professor William Ware in 1893. During this time Olmsted evolved his theories on environment in consequence of the great national population shifts from rural to urban areas and the enormous growth of industrialization. He was to see and write about the process of population concentration in urban centers, the lack of intelligent planning to meet this urban growth, the confused mixture in cities of mercantilism, communications, and land use, the consequent abandonment of cities for the suburbs by those who could afford to do so, and the deterioration of the urban core into crowded slums.

The plans he envisioned for the entire region, suggested in reports to the Brooklyn park commissioners in 1868, began with a comprehensive street and parkway system for Brooklyn that extended to the East River shore, bridged the river, and connected with a broad avenue leading to Central Park and the parks beyond it. This open space–broad boulevard network was to extend from the wide Atlantic beaches of Brooklyn to the Hudson Valley with its Palisade background. While Olmsted could do no comprehensive work of this sort apart from his parks and parkways, the results in Brooklyn show the nucleus of such a system, with Prospect Park at its center and Ocean and Eastern parkways reaching out from it, to be connected with the Coney Island shore in one

direction and the Queens park system in the other and to the more elaborate communications systems of the future. Olmsted's thought was that these parkways were to be used as access to the city's business centers from the "spacious and healthful" residential areas to be built up alongside them.

His later 1877 report on the 23rd and 24th wards in the Bronx also emphasized the need for generously spaced suburban-type housing, following the structure of the hilly, rolling land in these areas, avoiding the imposition of the grid plan as was later done, unfortunately, wherever possible. Whether designs of parks, parkways, urban or suburban entities, Olmsted conceived of them as facets of his comprehensive metropolitan ideal, aspects of which he was able to demonstrate more fully in other parts of the United States. Boston, for example, has this nation's first metropolitan-scale park and parkway system—Olmsted's gift to that city of an "emerald necklace" of open space, an urban treasure of incomparable value—while his ideas for the Bronx are embodied in his designs for beautiful suburbs like Baltimore's Roland Park or Chicago's Riverside.

Olmsted built and planned for New York City and for each of its boroughs; from a recreational area in Queens to what must have been perhaps one of the most comprehensive ecological-environmental presentations (for Staten Island) in the history of these things, by the man who, when counted as the philosophic father of our state and national park systems, is probably responsible for the betterment and preservation of more of the earth's

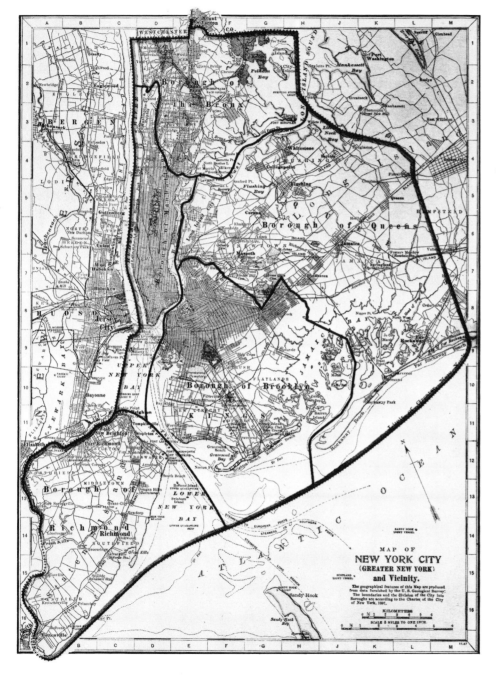

1. New York City in 1897, the metropolis finally consolidated by the combination of the cities of New York and Brooklyn, plus the counties of Queens, Staten Island, and the Bronx, the latter annexed from Westchester.

surface than anyone else. And this he accomplished not by auto-cratic or imperial fiat but by thousands of workaday presentations, plans, and reports given to officials, bureaucrats, politicians, and all manner of men in a democratic society.

Because of his prominence in the New York scene, Olmsted once even found himself a candidate for Vice-President of the United States in 1872 on the Independent Liberal Republican Party ticket together with William S. Groesbeck of Cincinnati. The *New York Times* report of June 22 on the convention held the day before at the Fifth Avenue Hotel was tentative in its evalu-ation: "... candidate for Vice President, Mr. Frederick Law Olm-sted of the city [is] a gentleman of high character whose prom-inent connection with national politics is so recent that we abstain from the endeavor to account for his nomination." Unwilling, but drafted because of his non-political (and therefore attractive) stature, Olmsted was protesting the choice of Horace Greeley as the principal candidate to oppose the incumbent Ulysses S. Grant; the same Horace Greeley who was counted among the illustrious New Yorkers who signed one of the petitions fifteen years earlier that recommended Olmsted for the job of superintendent of Cen-tral Park, the beginning of one of the most remarkable careers in all of American history.

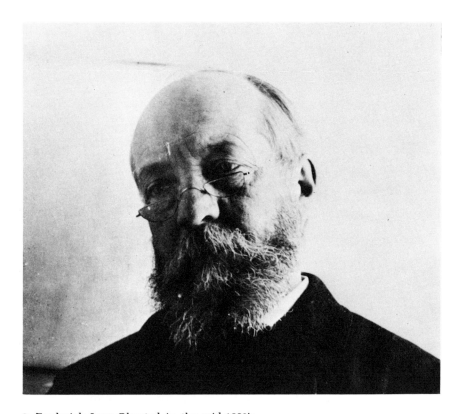

2. Frederick Law Olmsted in the mid-1890's.

3. An overview of the Central Park site in 1862, one of the earliest photographs after construction began.

4. A winter scene of the pond north of 59th Street in 1847, showing the desolate nature of the area destined to become Central Park. Gouache by R. Gignoux.

5. Squatters' shacks on park land, typical of colonies of this sort scattered over the site. Photo taken in 1862.

Authorization of a site for New York's first large public park from the State Legislature came in 1853 after agitation by many important New Yorkers, who held up European examples to emphasize the cultural void in an important and fast-growing metropolis. Apart from its sullen population in makeshift shanties, the site with its fields and rocky hillocks was hardly prepossessing. Clearing and preparing the area called for supervision by a capable man.

4

5

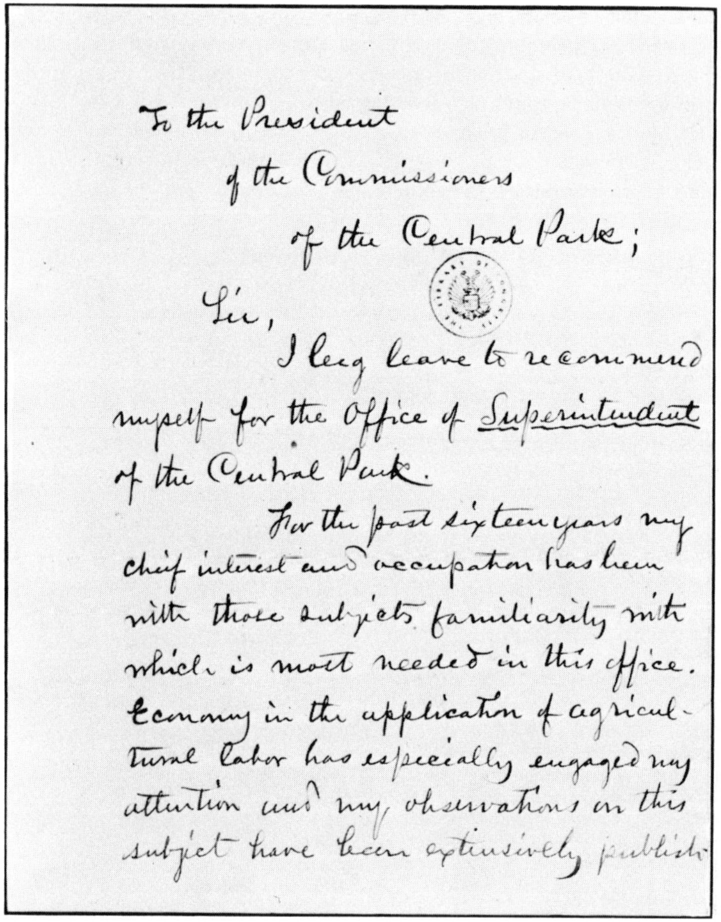

To the President
of the Commissioners
of the Central Park;
Sir,
I beg leave to recommend
myself for the Office of <u>Superintendent</u>
of the Central Park.

For the past sixteen years my
chief interest and occupation has been
with those subjects, familiarity with
which is most needed in this office.
Economy in the application of agricultural labor has especially engaged my
attention and my observations on this
subject have been extensively publish-

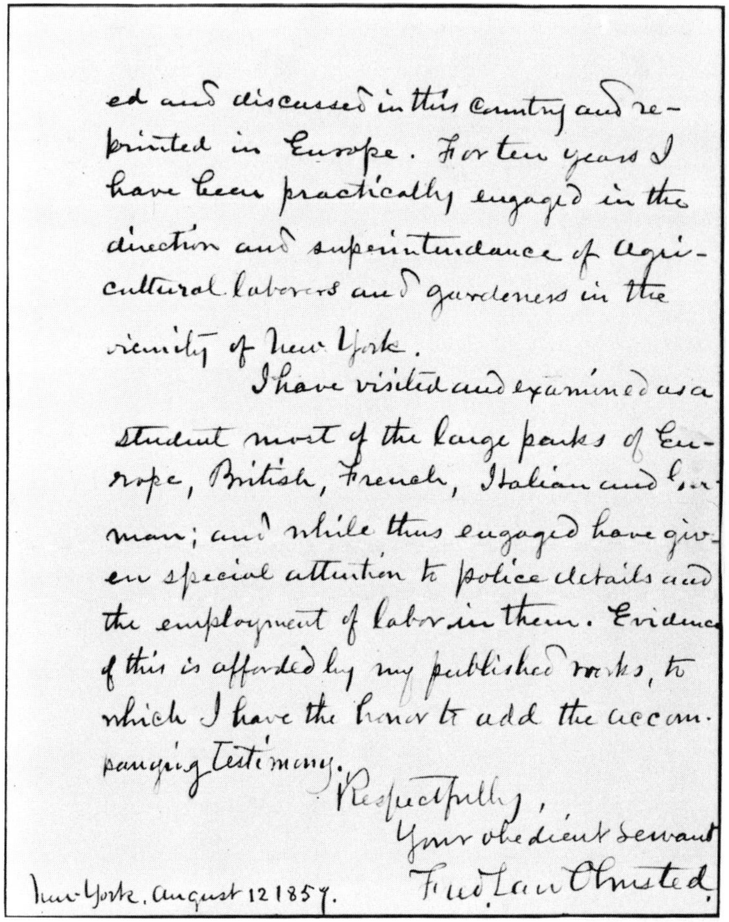

ed and discussed in this country and re-
printed in Europe. For ten years I
have been practically engaged in the
direction and superintendence of Agricultural laborers and gardeners in the
vicinity of New York.

I have visited and examined as a
student most of the large parks of Europe, British, French, Italian and Ger-
man; and while thus engaged have giv-
en special attention to police details and
the employment of labor in them. Evidence
of this is afforded by my published works, to
which I have the honor to add the accompanying testimony.
Respectfully,
Your obedient servant
Fred Law Olmsted.

New York. August 12 1857.

6

6. Olmsted's letter to the commissioners of Central Park.

7. Frederick Law Olmsted in about the mid-1860's.

7

8

9

8. Competition announcement in the *New York Herald,* October 30, 1857: Plans for the Central Park.

9. One of a pair of photographs of the site of Central Park looking south from 110th Street, probably taken in the late 1850's.

10. Another view of the site at the same time by photographer G. Rockwood.

10

Beginning with Central Park in 1857 and continuing for the next three decades, Olmsted and Vaux worked on a full range of environmental projects that included urban and national parks, residential developments, and public and private landscape designs. Their collaboration, while intermittent, was cordial, Olmsted always making certain during his lifetime that Vaux's brilliance as an architect-designer-planner was recognized and credited.

12

11. Calvert Vaux, 1868.

12. Frederick Law Olmsted, c. 1860.

13a

14a

13a. Humphrey Repton's sketch of "Wembly,
before improvements."

13b. "Wembly, after improvements," Repton's
landscape design, 1794.

14a. Country roadway, before.

14b. Country roadway, after.

13b

14b

Before and after scenes by Humphrey Repton, one of the greatest English landscape designers. Olmsted was tremendously affected by English pastoral landscapes, which became the basis for many of the vistas in his American urban park designs. He used the same before and after illustration technique in his "Greensward" competition entry with Calvert Vaux.

21

22

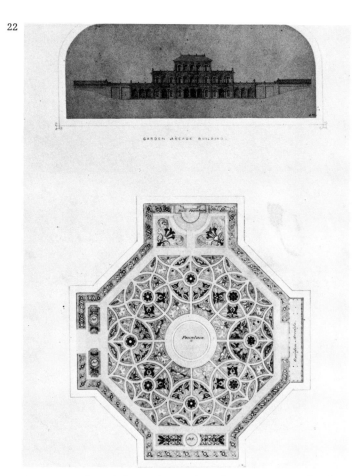

21. Greensward Presentation Sketch No. 1, the lake, before and after.

22. Greensward Presentation Sketch No. 11, the garden arcade building and flower garden plan.

23. Greensward Presentation Sketch No. 9, before and after, panorama and viewing tower.

A group selected from the series of presentation sketches accompanying the Greensward Plan drawing by Olmsted and Vaux, delivered to the park commissioners in 1858. They won the competition and the $2,000 prize.

23

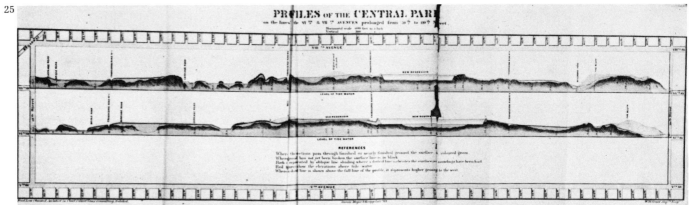

24. The Promenade, looking south toward the Arsenal, 1858.

25. Geological profiles of the long axis. Olmsted and Vaux carefully considered the site topography within which they created their own rational earth sculpture.

26. The Promenade (Mall) under construction, 1858. Ten million horsecart loads of earth were transported into and out of the park during its construction.

27. Geological profile of the short axis.

26

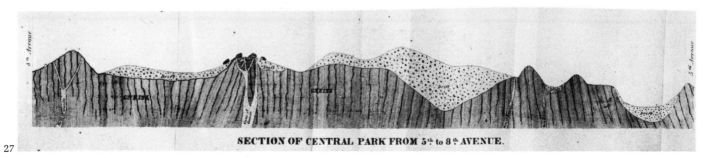

SECTION OF CENTRAL PARK FROM 5ᵗʰ to 8ᵗʰ AVENUE.

27

Central Park was the scene of civil engineering on a grand scale during its construction. Olmsted writes of supervising almost 4,000 men at work at one time.

28

29

28. Construction of the water system for draining and filling the lake. Photo taken in 1862.

29. Excavation and construction in the park as seen looking northwest from the corner of Fifth Avenue and 58th Street. Photo taken about 1860.

30. The new large central reservoir under construction in 1862, around which Olmsted and Vaux made their design.

30

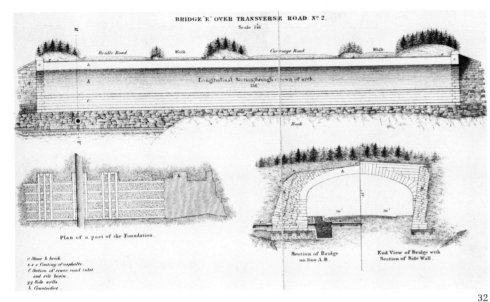

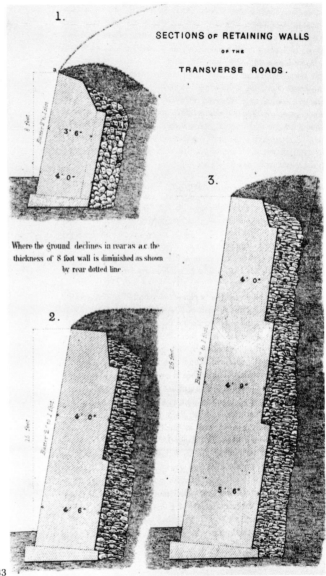

32

31. Tunnel carved out through Vista Rock for Transverse Road No. 2 at 79th Street.

32. Bridge "E" over Transverse Road No. 2.

33. Transverse Road retaining walls section.

33

Necessary and noisy cross-traffic carried on the transverse roadways is screened by trees and plantings from the park proper. Olmsted's four separate circulation systems—no less sophisticated for its time than Le Corbusier's seven levels of circulation—have been functioning successfully for about 110 years.

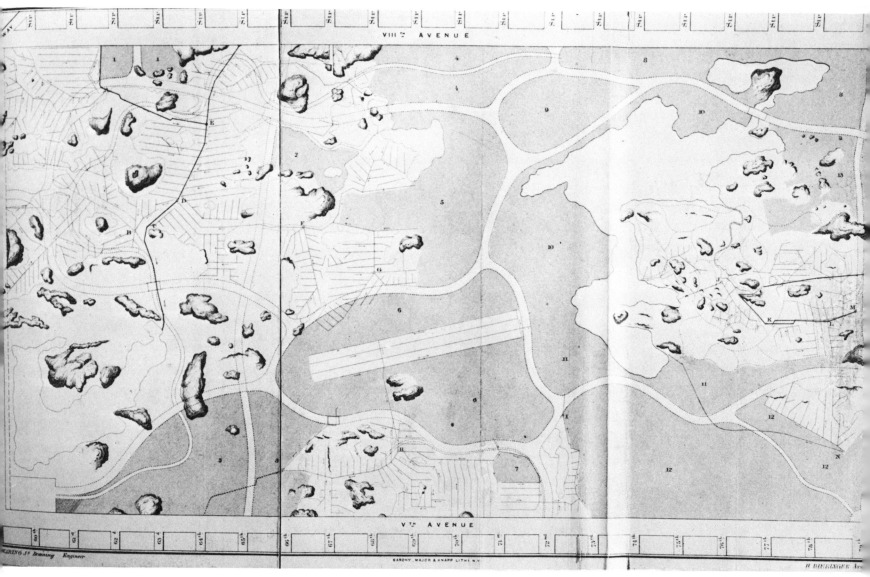

Olmsted and Vaux designed still another circulation system, below ground and more extensive than that for traffic. It was partly based on Olmsted's agricultural experience and on park maintenance information he acquired in England.

35

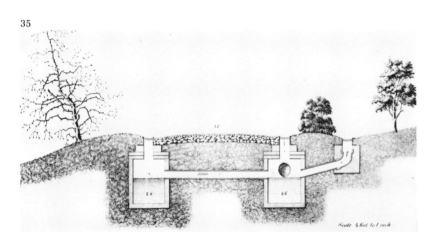

36

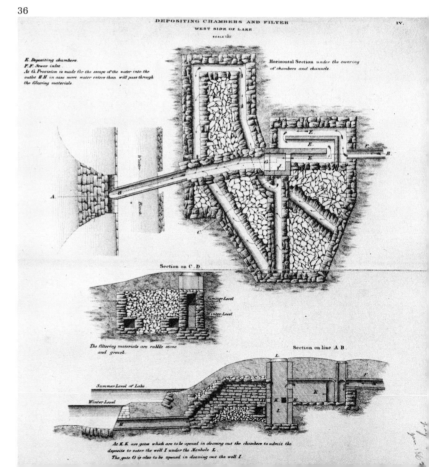

34. Diagram of the drainage system of the lower portion of the park as of December, 1858. The black line network indicates underground channels.

35. Drainage method for pathway.

36. Depositing chambers and filter, west side of lake. The chambers must be emptied periodically of the debris carried into them by the channels that drain off rainwater.

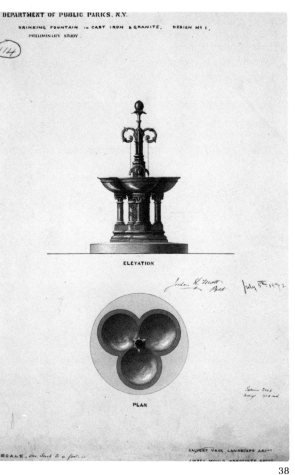

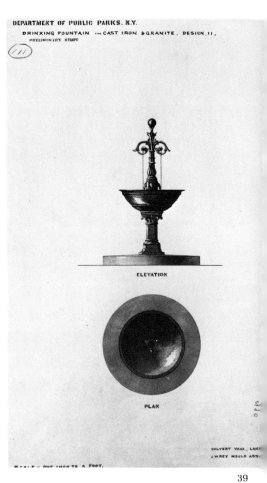

37

38

39

37, 38, 39, 40. Designs for drinking fountains in the parks. Note Olmsted's approval on the sketch for the Union Square fountain.

41. "The Water Fountain," Central Park. Photo taken in the 1880's.

41

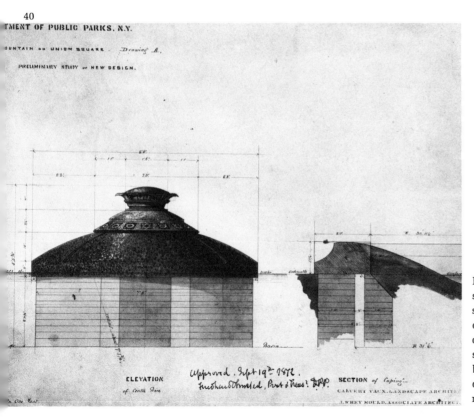

40

TMENT OF PUBLIC PARKS, N.Y.

UNTAIN on UNION SQUARE.   Drawing A.

PRELIMINARY STUDY of NEW DESIGN.

ELEVATION
of Centre Pier

Approved. Sept 19th 1872.
Frederick Olmsted, Prest & Treas? D.P.P.

SECTION of Coping.

CALVERT VAUX, LANDSCAPE ARCHITECT

J. WREY MOULD, ASSOCIATE ARCHITECT

During their tenure in charge of construction of the park, Olmsted and Vaux designed and supervised the construction of structures, furniture, and fittings for Central Park as well as other New York City parks. The architect Jacob Wrey Mould collaborated with Calvert Vaux and Olmsted in many of the structures, bridges, terraces, arches, stairways, fountains, benches, masonry work, fences, gates, lamp posts, mosaic designs, and innumerable details of every description that needed to be drawn for fabrication.

PRELIMINARY STUDY.

Nº I.
Wrought & Iron
with Lamps.

Nº II.
Wood & Iron.

Nº III.
Wood only.

Nº IV.
Wood only.

42

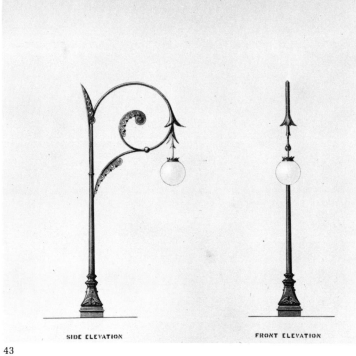

SIDE ELEVATION

FRONT ELEVATION

43

42, 43, 44, 45, 46, 47. Designs for lamps and
park furniture.

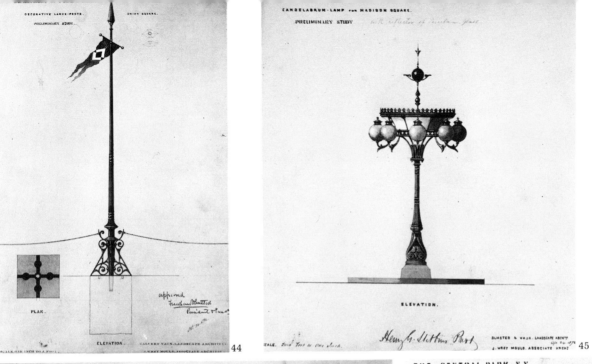

DECORATIVE LANCE-POSTS.

PRELIMINARY STUDY.

UNION SQUARE.

PLAN.

ELEVATION.

ELEVATION.

44

45

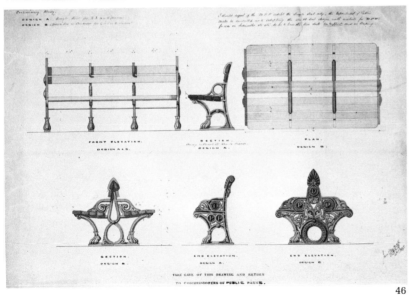

FRONT ELEVATION.

SECTION.

PLAN.

SECTION.

END ELEVATION.

END ELEVATION.

TAKE CARE OF THIS DRAWING AND RETURN
TO COMMISSIONERS OF PUBLIC PARKS.

46

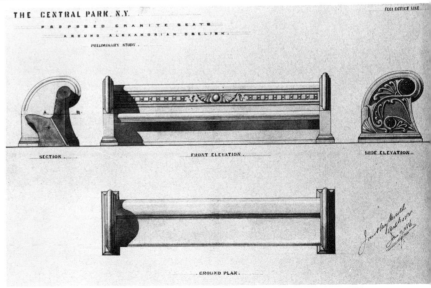

THE CENTRAL PARK, N.Y.

PROPOSED GRANITE SEATS

AROUND ALEXANDRIAN OBELISK.

PRELIMINARY STUDY.

SECTION.

FRONT ELEVATION.

SIDE ELEVATION.

GROUND PLAN.

47

49

48. View of Greensward just before the Trefoil Arch, the area just northeast of the Esplanade (later the Bethesda Fountain area). The park was just coming into being as this photo was taken, about 1860.

49. "View of the Lake and Terrace Looking South," one of a set of twelve lithographs of the Park by G. W. Fasel in 1862.

50. "View of the Lake Looking West," lithograph by G. W. Fasel.

51. Map of Central Park, 1873.

52. A view of the Esplanade in about 1860. The trees in the foreground had just been planted, and the photograph shows nature only just beginning to fill in the forms outlined by Olmsted and Vaux.

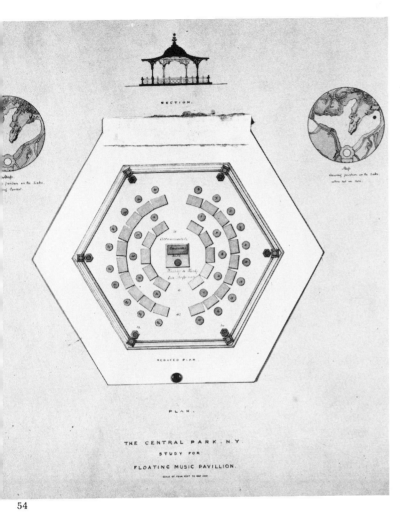

53. "Central Park, New York—Music on the Lake," *Harper's Weekly,* October 14, 1865.

54. Study for a floating music pavilion in the lake at the Esplanade.

55. Central Park sheet music published by H. B. Dodworth, New York, 1863.

56

56. "View of Terrace and Lake, Central Park, New York," *Appleton's Journal*, June 18, 1870.

57. Letter to Olmsted from Andrew Haswell Green.

58. "The Hamburg Swans," *Harper's Weekly*, July 27, 1857.

Central Park achieved immense popularity in no time at all. By far the most attractive place in all of New York, it became the subject of frequent reports in the journals of the day, the setting for novels, short stories, and moral essays, the site for celebrations, parades, picnics, games, festivals, riding, boating, promenading, and romance. It filled a heretofore enormous void the city never knew it had. It emptied the grog shops on Sundays and was the object of treasured gifts by the city's young and old; the Park Reports of 1865 listed a variety of gifts to the menagerie: May 25, One Opposum [D]* presented by a Lady; June 7, One Gray Squirrel, presented by Master Alonzo Dayton; Seven White Mice, presented by Master D. M. Hagadorn; and so forth. *Dead.

Board of Commissioners of the Central Park,

OFFICE, BANK OF COMMERCE BUILDINGS,

New York, May 11th 1860

Sir

Twelve Swans were to leave Hamburgh in the Steamer Bavaria on the 8th inst, they will probably be here about the 26th inst. A person will accompany them. I send herewith a plan received from the Hamburgh Consul of the mode of constructing nests for the Swans, and also his letter, which please read and return here.

Yours respy

Andw H Green

Comptroller of the Park

Fred Law Olmsted Esq
Architect in chief & Supt
Central Park

57

58

CENTRAL PARK IN WINTER.

60

59. "Winter in Central Park," *Harper's Weekly,*
January 30, 1864.

60. "Sleighing in Central Park," *Harper's
Weekly,* February 27, 1886.

CENTRAL PARK—THE DANGERS THAT THREATEN IT.—Drawn by Thomas Worth.

CENTRAL PARK.

When the custody of the public parks of this ... was taken from a non-partisan commission ... placed in the hands of politicians, it was ...phesied that the result would be a general dete-

The worst apprehensions have been realized. This is most noticeable in Central Park. Under the old régime it was one of the most beautiful parks in the world. The walks, drives, and lawns were kept in perfect order, and every year saw new features of beauty added to its old at-

all been changed. Everything suffers; lawns, drives, and walks have deteriorated. The shrubbery and the flower beds are no longer what they used to be. Beautiful trees of many years' growth have been cut down to facilitate fast driving, and this in ground where fast driving ought to be

bring the Park back to the condition it was when it fell into the hands of a political co... mission. Meanwhile the Park Commissioners ... pend their energies in wrangling among the selves. Perhaps this is well: if they d... n they might do more injury to the Park than

61

Thomas Nast, illustrating in *Harper's,* covers a successful protest against an incursion attempt into the park by a "World's Fair." Other attempts did and do succeed however, against this "empty" land, productive of nothing, except the regeneration of the human mind and spirit.

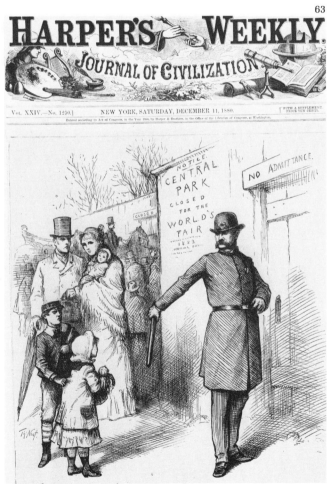

64

64, 65, 66. Photographer J. S. Johnston captures a variety of moods in Central Park in 1894. The Mall with its lush canopy, the Bethesda Fountain and pathway leading to the Trefoil Arch, and the Gondola.

65

67

68

67, 68, 69, 70. Stereoscopic Views in the
People's Pleasure Ground.

COPYRIGHT 1889, by UNDERWOOD&UNDERWOOD. A Thousand skaters, Central Park N.Y. (Instantaneous)

69

"Limited Express"—Railway in Central Park, New York City, U.S.A.

70

71

72

108

71. "Dove Cot," 1862.
72. "Evergreen Walk East of Ramble," 1862.
73. "Bird Cage on Mall," 1860.
74. A rustic arbor of the 1880's.

73

74

75

RULES AND CONDITIONS
OF SERVICE OF
THE CENTRAL PARK KEEPERS.

No keeper, having been instructed to occupy a post or beat, shall leave the same until he is regularly relieved by another keeper, except by special orders from a superior officer, or except it is clearly necessary, and only for so long a time as may be necessary, in order to secure an offender.

No keeper shall bring, receive or drink ardent spirits when on the Park, and no keeper shall frequent taverns or tippling-houses, or become intoxicated when off the Park.

No keeper shall intentionally or knowingly screen, nor, unless prevented by special or more important duty, neglect to apprehend, or report any offender, of whom he may have knowledge, against the laws, or against the ordinances of the Board of Commissioners of the Central Park, or against the rules for the government of those employed in the construction of the Park, and no man shall conceal or attempt to conceal any neglect of duty or disobedience of orders or rules, either by himself or by any other keeper or officer of the Park.

Any keeper who shall act in disregard of the above prohibitions shall at the end of the half-day on which the act of disregard occurred cease to exercise the duties, to occupy the station and to wear the uniform of a keeper of the Central Park; and if he continue to occupy such station, wear such uniform, and perform such duties, he shall not be entitled to pay for the same, and any claim he shall make for remuneration for services as a keeper of the Park from the date of his neglect of these prohibitions shall be deemed fraudulent; provided, however, that if he shall faithfully, truly and honestly write, without unnecessary delay, to the Superintendent of the Park, stating fully the circumstances under which such neglect of duty occurred, and the reasons for it, and the Superintendent shall see fit thereupon to order him again on duty as a keeper of the Park, he shall thereafter again be entitled to pay.

Unless otherwise specially required, each man when on patrol duty shall preserve himself and his garments clean and neat, and in accordance with the special orders as to uniform and dress; he shall be seriously attentive to his duty, and not place himself in a position where vigilance and watchfulness are impracticable, but shall carry himself erect, according to the instructions received at drill, and march at a quick step from one part of his beat to another, except when it is necessary to move slowly or to halt entirely for the observation required in his duty, or for the detection or apprehension of offenders. He shall not converse with those employed on the Park unless necessarily and only so far as is necessary with regard to their duty or his own duty. He shall not converse with visitors unless first addressed by them, and only for the purpose of giving such information as they may require with regard to the Park. He shall not stand at one point or in one part of his beat more than five minutes at a time in conversation with any visitor or party of visitors. He shall use no profane language, or harsh, exasperating or unnecessary disrespectful language in the execution of duty, but shall as far as possible preserve a quiet, reserved and vigilant manner. When he sees occasion to warn, instruct or order any persons on the Park, he shall do so, as far as possible, kindly and respectfully.

In all other respects, he shall observe and be governed by the rules and customs of subordination and discipline usual in military organizations so far as he shall be instructed in the same.

Sergeants on duty are forbidden to speak to or with the men, except on matters of their duty. Men on duty are forbidden to speak to sergeants or other men, except on matters of their duty.

Men on duty intending to address a sergeant, an officer, or another man on duty, will first salute him by raising a hand to the front of the cap, without bending the neck or body. This formality is intended as a check upon intercourse which might otherwise lead to neglect of duty. It is in all cases to be returned, and neglect to return the salute is to be considered not only a personal affront but a disregard of the habits of discipline required by the Board, and is to be reported in a special report to the Superintendent.

A sergeant or an acting sergeant is to be constantly at the office on office duty. The duty of the office-sergeant, besides that of drilling the men, as may be specially ordered, and besides his general duties as sergeant, shall be to receive and record complaints, to record arrests, to give information to any calling for it, to prevent persons without business from remaining at the station, to prevent any one but keepers, the house-keeper or door-men and officers of the Park from entering the keepers' room, to prevent keepers from lounging in the office, to prevent excessive noise in the keepers' room, to watch the clock and see that all duties are punctually performed so far as the station is concerned, and that every man is prepared in time for his regular duties; to see that reports are properly and punctually made, and especially to see that no keeper leaves the keepers' room for any purpose, unless he is off duty, without being perfectly clean, hair brushed, beard combed or evidently shaven, within twenty-four hours, and in full uniform in every particular, cloth clean, brass polished, shoes clean and newly oiled or polished, coat buttoned to the neck and no white collar visible, gloves clean. Keepers or, acting keepers not uniformed are to be inspected in all other particulars except those of the uniform. No keeper is to be allowed to remain in the office, or to pass through it, or to go out at the outer door on any duty, who has not been inspected, and who has not passed inspection satisfactorily. Keepers off duty are not to be allowed to pass out wearing any part of their uniform.

If the sergeant on office duty is under a necessity to leave the office, and no other sergeant is ready to relieve him, he shall appoint a keeper to act in his place, who shall perform all the above described duties of office sergeant, and be respected as office sergeant until relieved by a sergeant.

Whenever there are two or more keepers of the reserve at the station, one shall be constantly ready in all respects for any duty, and shall be in the office, and a second shall be dressed and ready at once to take the place of the first if he should, while waiting, be required to leave the office, but the sergeant may permit the second to be in the keepers' room. This duty shall be taken in turn by each man. The first shall be called the "Office-Keeper," and the second the "Office Relief." When the "office-keeper" is relieved the next man in turn shall immediately dress, and within two minutes report himself for inspection to the office sergeant as the office relief. The office-keeper may read, but shall not fall asleep, or smoke, or enter into conversation with any one while on this duty. The office relief, while in the keepers' room, need be under no constraint, except as to wearing his entire body-uniform. He may remove his cap and gloves after inspection, putting them on again when called to relieve the office-keeper.

FRED. LAW OLMSTED,
Superintendent.

76 MARCH 12TH, 1859.

75. Mounted police in Central Park, 1895.
76. "Rules and Conditions of Service of the Central Park Keepers," 1859.
77. A lawn-littered afternoon in about 1900.

77

78. "When I come to my Park, and get away from people and houses and discords, I feel Nature elevate me, strengthen me, fill me with a fresh courage and faith. I feel all these things with an overwhelming intensity.

79. "There is the glory of the city—that is one thing. There is the glory of the Park—that is another thing.... There are times when I love to stand at the juncture of two great avenues and feel the tide of human life beat up against me...times when the clang of the cable cars, the rumble of the stages...the shrill whistle of the post-man, are as music to my ears. But I know also the charm of Nature, her great still-ness, her majestic aloofness; know the value and refreshment of wide vistas. Do you know the muscles of your eye need stretching now and then just as all your muscles do? The two influences—that of the town and that of Nature—respond to different needs. They should be kept apart. Where combination or compromise is ef-fected, there is certain to be failure."

From Annie Nathan Meyer,
My Park Book, 1898

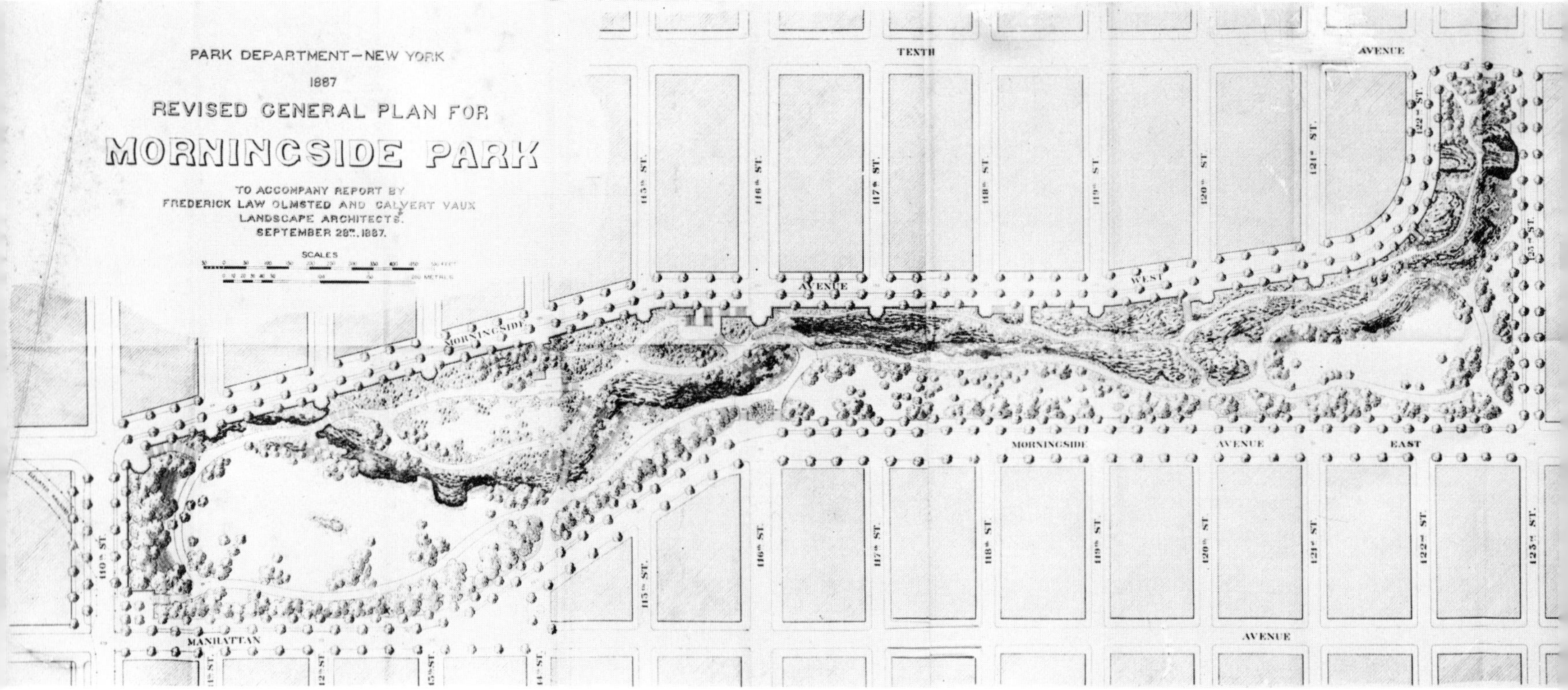

PARK DEPARTMENT—NEW YORK
1887
REVISED GENERAL PLAN FOR
MORNINGSIDE PARK
TO ACCOMPANY REPORT BY
FREDERICK LAW OLMSTED AND CALVERT VAUX
LANDSCAPE ARCHITECTS.
SEPTEMBER 28ᵀᴴ, 1887.

SCALES

80

80. Revised plan for Morningside Park, 1887. The first report was written in 1873.

81. The rocky cliffside before 1873.

82. Morningside Park in 1900 with the crossing arches of The Cathedral of St. John the Divine seen under construction at the left of the photograph.

Morningside Park, mostly a cliffside, is one of the more typical examples of land "left over" because speculators and builders could not use it. It was then presented to Olmsted and Vaux to be made into a park, which they did, Olmsted protesting the lack of any sort of plan with regard to the city's park placement and use.

Civilizing cities in spite of themselves, Olmsted and his partners could take cliffs in Manhattan, mountains in Montreal, and marshes in Boston and turn them into the loveliest of parks, treasures of open space.

81

82

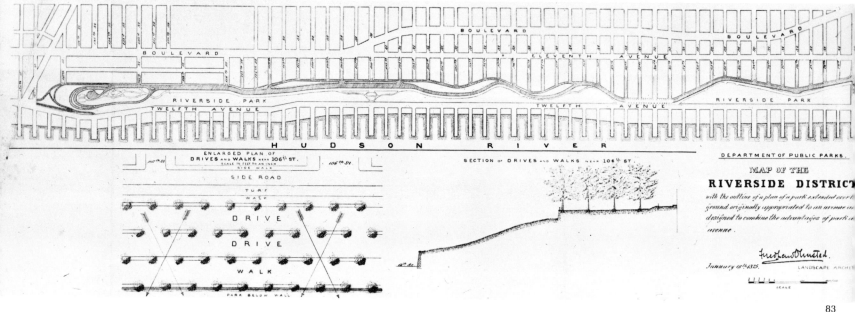

83

83. Map of the Riverside District, 1875.

84. Riverside Drive, the Hudson River, and the
New Jersey Palisades, from the cover of a
promotional booklet of 1888 describing the
merits of Manhattan's upper west side as
a residential neighborhood.

In his official park capacity, Olmsted was also responsible to the park
commission for "laying-out" the land being developed in upper Manhattan and the Bronx. His ideas, far in advance of the time, urban
planning in the true sense, were rejected in favor of the visible profit
square-lot grid-plan system.

Doing what he could in the Riverside District of upper Manhattan's
west side, Olmsted inserted a park into the grid: ". . . the Department
was advised, in 1873, that the imaginary line by which the site for the
avenue was divided from the site for the park should be disregarded,
and a plan prepared, with a view to utilize, in the greatest degree prac-
ticable, the advantages offered by the territory, *as a whole,* for the
several purposes—first, of a means of access to the property on its
east side; second, of a pleasure drive, commanding a fine view over
the river, airy and shaded; third, of a foot promenade, commanding the
same view, and also airy and shaded."

84

RIVERSIDE
DRIVE

Riverside Drive near 40 x 94 th street

85

85. Squatters' shacks in the Riverside District, drawing by Thomas R. Manley, 1892.

86. Riverside Park area, about 1900.

87. Riverside Drive at 94th Street, about 1890.

Olmsted's design is evident in the curved drive following topographic contours. Further north from 104th to 110th Street, the original design (Fig. 83) shows traffic divisions for carriages, equestrians, bicycles, and pedestrians.

87

88

89

The policy of conducting interments or at least placing monuments in public parks is unfortunately still a current one in New York City. Olmsted, asked to advise on Grant's Tomb, responded: "The space available reaches from the end of the Terrace to the brow of a declivity from which a magnificent view is commanded up the valley of the Hudson...The site proposed for the Grant sepulchre is on a line, and about midway, between the end of the terrace already built and this point of view. It occupies the centre of the ground reserved for the terminal feature of the Promenade. It is a very fine site for a public monument. But it will be extremely unfortunate if, on the one hand, the remains of the dead are brought into close association with the gayety of the Promenade at this culminating point."

88. Grant's Tomb, Riverside Park, 1912.

89. "Present Appearance of the Interior of the Temporary Tomb of General Grant at Riverside Park," *Frank Leslie's Illustrated*, August 29, 1885.

90. "Troop 99, Uptown Branch of Boy Scouts of America, Tree Patrol of Riverside Park," 1926. Olmsted trained "keepers" and established rules for them. This tree patrol would have earned his approval. Is there a lesson for today? Parks simply cannot patrol or maintain themselves.

90

91. The Battle Pass, Photo in 1865. The Revolutionary War site within the bounds of Prospect Park, the area typical of Brooklyn farmland.

92. Calvert Vaux's original sketch plan of the site, sent to Olmsted in California. The Viele plan consists of the solid outline areas bisected by Flatbush Avenue; the dotted line extension (upper right) is Vaux's.

91

Perhaps the most satisfying experience that Olmsted and Vaux shared was their work in Brooklyn. Here, securing greater understanding and cooperation, Olmsted was able to work on Prospect Park and its connected Parkways in accord with some of the urban precepts he proposed earlier for Manhattan, rejected as fanciful.

Portions of Prospect Park embody in places the considered maturity that the tour-de-force of Central Park lacks. The preliminary layout by Vaux, who recommended a major boundary change, enabled the partners to achieve a single integrated whole in equilibrium, a broad lake on one side balanced by a grand, rolling meadow on the other, with a series of felicitous pastoral variations in between.

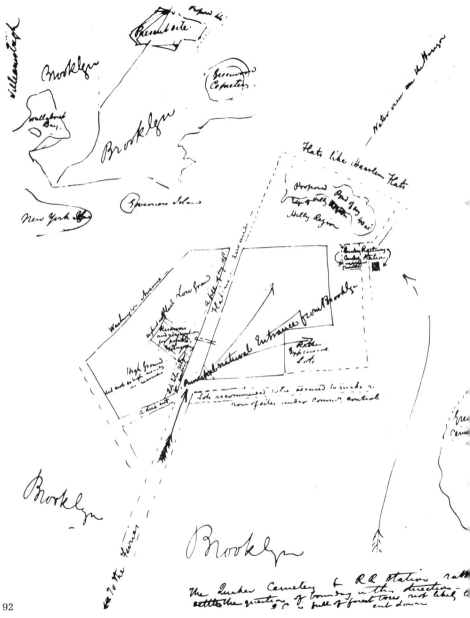

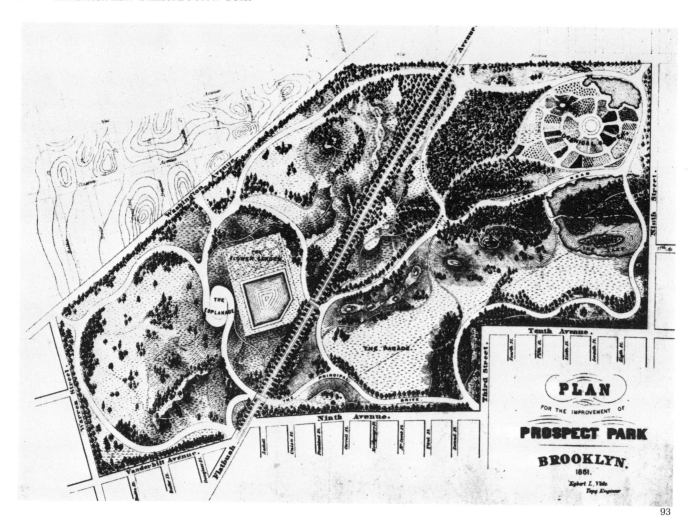

93

93. Egbert Viele's Prospect Park plan.

94. Olmsted, Vaux and Company's Prospect
Park plan.

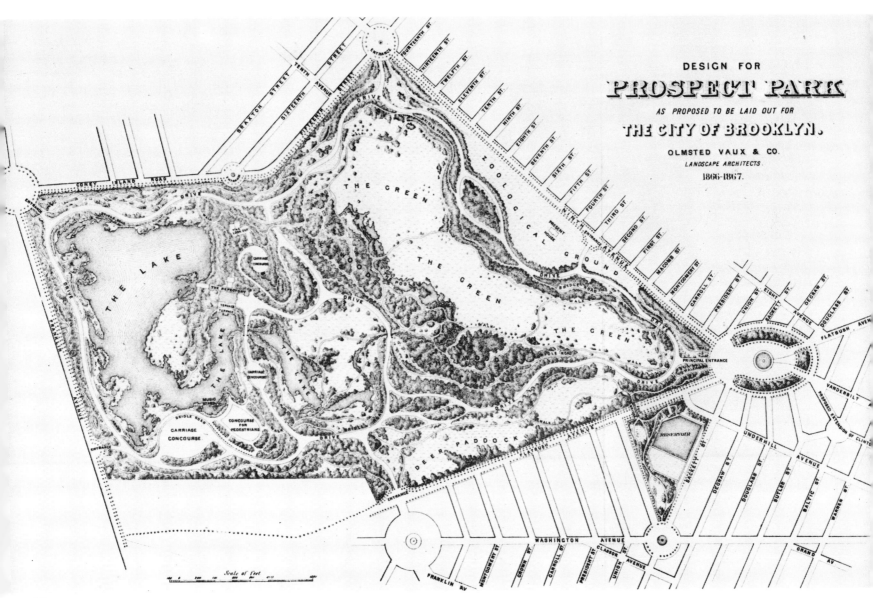

DESIGN FOR

PROSPECT PARK

AS PROPOSED TO BE LAID OUT FOR

THE CITY OF BROOKLYN.

OLMSTED VAUX & CO.
LANDSCAPE ARCHITECTS.
1866-1867.

95. Original appearance of the Prospect Park site. Photograph about 1865.

96. Surveying the site. It has been suggested that the two persons holding the drawing sheet are Vaux, on the left, and Olmsted, on the right. Photograph about 1865.

97. Tree-moving machine, Prospect Park.

98. Surveyors' camp in Prospect Park.

99. Construction in the park in 1867. The enormous pyramidal mounds could be top soil stored in the lake bed for replacement when excavation is completed.

97

98

99

It should now be understood that the major parks of New York did not come into existence simply by having fences built around them. Containing everything from important works of civil and hydraulic engineering to carefully planned seasonal shades of green, they reflect the patient aesthetic judgment of the time.

100

100. "Prospect Park, Brooklyn," *Appleton's Journal*, June 4, 1870.

101. An early view, overlooking the Vale of Cashmere. The word paradise relates to the Persian word for park, enclosure.

102. The Long Meadow in 1902.
103. Deer in Prospect Park, 1870's.

103

104

105

104. Rustic shelter near the Meadowport Arch.

105. Terrace of Pedestrian Concourse, near the Music Grove.

106. Lawn tennis, a removable activity; the nets are picked up and taken away to be replaced by croquet, bowling, or a Maypole, leaving a versatile space, not one dedicated to single sporting activities requiring permanent sheets of cement and wire net fences. Photos taken in 1885.

106

107

108

109

107. The Meadowport Arch.

108. The Nethermead Arches. Converging under them from left to right: bridle path, flowing stream, and pedestrian way; over these three is the carriage road.

109. The Cleftridge Span.

110. Brooklyn Park Commissioner George V. Brower and staff in front of their Litchfield Villa Headquarters in Prospect Park, 1897.

111. The Circular Yacht, a waterborne merry-go-round that operated on the pond.

112. "Design for the Pavilion to be erected in the Concert Grove," 1873. An elegant example of Victorian orientalia whose roof shape still survives.

113. Rustic Arbor. A good place to rest.

111

110

112

Rustic Arbor, Prospect Park.

113

ON THE LONG MEADOW.

CROQUET AND LAWN TENNIS.

Park Games.

114   115

TILIA EUROPEA.
EUROPEAN LINDEN.

ULMUS AMERICANA.
(NELLIE TREE), AMERICAN ELM.

114, 115, 116, 117. Vocabulary of a park.

VIEW TROUGH THE NETHER-MEAD ARCH.

CLEFT RIDGE ARCH.

Nether Mead Arches.

116

117

Scenery on Large Lake, Prospect Park.

118. At one odd moment in Brooklyn history a
corner of Prospect Park seems to have
been turned into a garbage dump. This
photograph was taken in 1900 by George
Brainard, whose glass negative collection
is carefully preserved and documented at
the Brooklyn Public Library.

119. An early vista through the Cleftridge Span. The choice offered by these two pictures of Prospect Park is not as clear to many people as one would like to think. A surprising number might find it arguable.

120. "Design for laying out Tompkins Park—
Brooklyn." Olmsted, Vaux and Co., Landscape Architects.

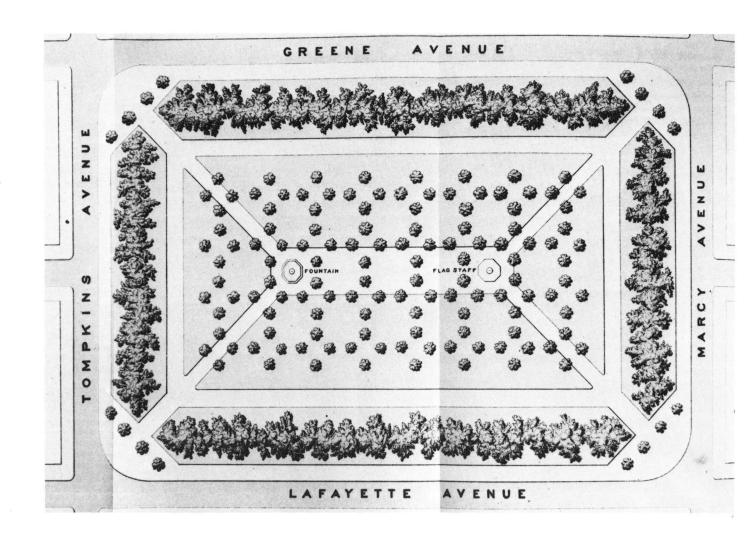

121. "Design for laying out the grounds known as Fort Greene or Washington Park, in the city of Brooklyn." Olmsted, Vaux and Co., Landscape Architects.

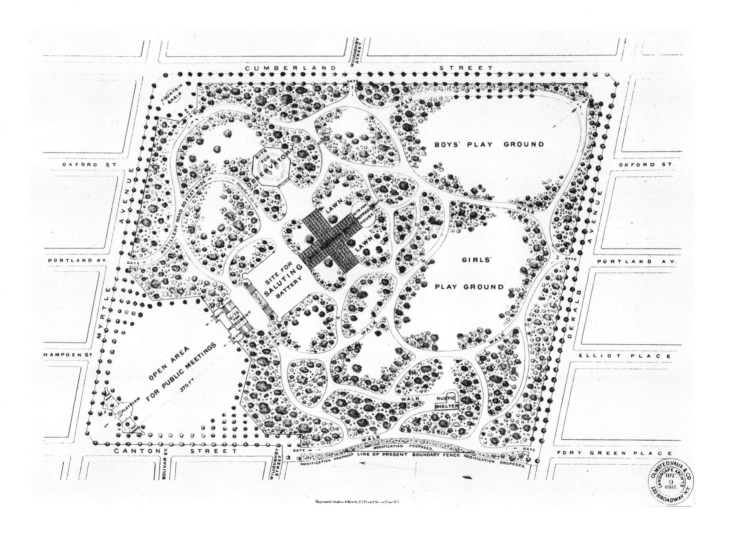

122

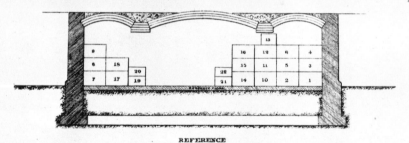

123

SECTION OF MARTYRS' MEMORIAL.

SHOWING POSITION OF THE REMAINS OF THE MARTYRS OF THE REVOLUTION
WITH INSCRIPTIONS ON THE COFFINS, SO FAR AS KNOWN,
NOW DEPOSITED IN THE VAULT AT FORT GREENE.

REFERENCE

1	Unknown	12	Rhode Island
2	,,	13	Drummer Boy.
3	,,	14	Virginia.
4	,,	15	Maryland.
5	,,	16	North Carolina.
6	,,	17	Connecticut.
7	,,	18	New Jersey.
8	Delaware	19	Georgia.
9	Major Benjamin Romaine	20	New York
10	Massachusetts	21	South Carolina
11	Pennsylvania	22	New Hampshire

Scale ½ inch · 1 foot

Of two urban parks in Brooklyn designed by Olmsted and Vaux, Tompkins Park is currently (1972) the scene of building construction, taking the form of a large concrete structure to serve as a Golden Age Center, although there are many acres of empty land around the park. The larger Fort Greene Park, initially designed to serve a variety of civic functions, contains an impressive number of dead in its funerary vault, expressing once again the unfortunate Victorian taste for intermixing cemetery and park.

124

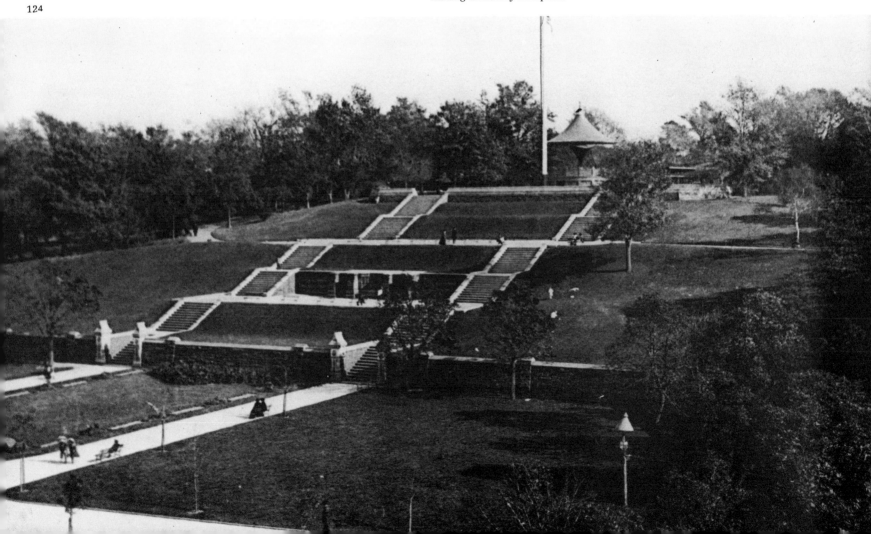

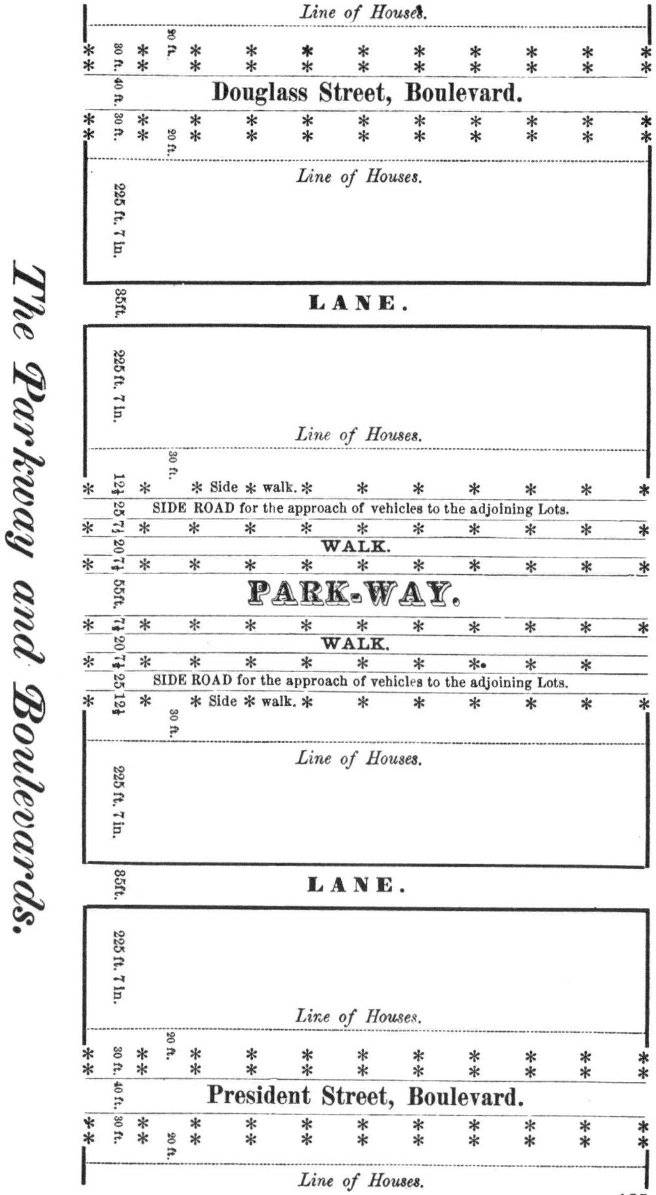

Line of Houses.

30 ft. 30 ft.

Douglass Street, Boulevard.

30 ft. 20 ft.

Line of Houses.

225 ft. 7 in.

L A N E .

85 ft.

225 ft. 7 in.

Line of Houses.

30 ft.

12¼ 25 7¼ * Side * walk. *

SIDE ROAD for the approach of vehicles to the adjoining Lots.

25 7¼ 20 **W A L K.**

PARK-WAY.

55 7¼

20 **W A L K.**

25 SIDE ROAD for the approach of vehicles to the adjoining Lots.

25 12¼ * Side * walk. *

30 ft.

Line of Houses.

225 ft. 7 in.

L A N E .

85 ft.

225 ft. 7 in.

Line of Houses.

30 ft. 30 ft.

President Street, Boulevard.

40 ft. 30 ft. 30 ft.

Line of Houses.

125

125. The Eastern Parkway system design, with details and subsidiary streets, diagram published in 1873.

126. Facsimile of title page showing the first printed use of the word parkway, "Report to the Prospect Park Commissioners," 1868.

127. Eastern Parkway begins at the oval plaza entrance to Prospect Park. Ocean Parkway begins at the upper boundary of the park.

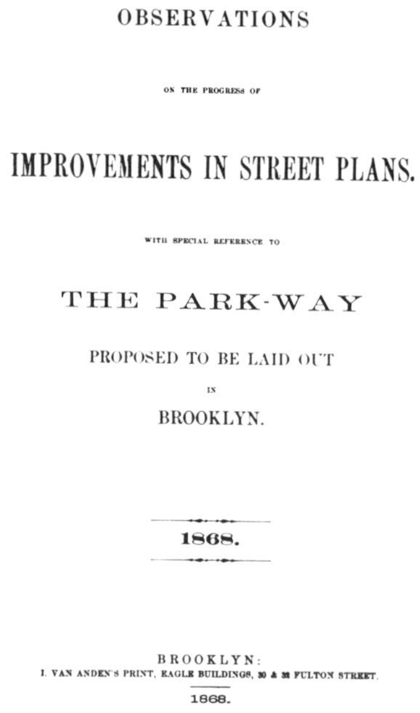

OBSERVATIONS

ON THE PROGRESS OF

IMPROVEMENTS IN STREET PLANS.

WITH SPECIAL REFERENCE TO

THE PARK-WAY

PROPOSED TO BE LAID OUT

IN

BROOKLYN.

1868.

BROOKLYN:
I. VAN ANDEN'S PRINT, EAGLE BUILDINGS, 30 & 38 FULTON STREET.
1868.

126

Inventing the word and elaborating the "parkway" in their 1868 report, Olmsted and Vaux went beyond their earlier and simpler Ocean Parkway and designed Eastern Parkway as part of a sophisticated arterial-residential complex. Park, parkway, and residential area were now functioning facets of a greater whole that Olmsted had in mind and wrote about, but which he was not to achieve in New York.

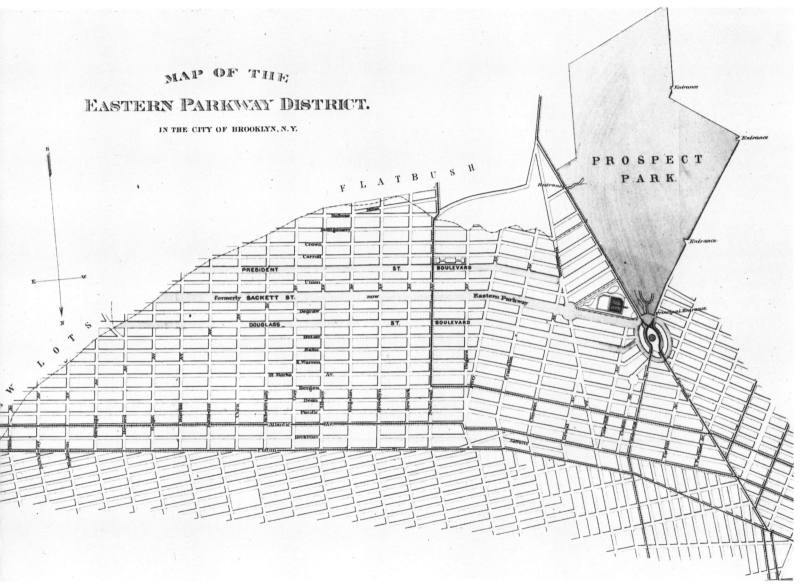

MAP OF THE

EASTERN PARKWAY DISTRICT.

IN THE CITY OF BROOKLYN, N.Y.

PROSPECT PARK.

FLATBUSH

Eastern Parkway

127

129

On October 27, 1898, Winston Buzby, defying the law, attempted to drive an automobile into Central Park. Forbidden because of the danger to horses in the parks, the automobile was not considered a pleasure vehicle by the authorities. This test case, however, went in favor of the car, and in the next year the first permit to drive in Central Park was issued to Mr. Robert Smith. An earlier, more peaceful era was partially recaptured when, in 1966, cars were banned in the parks on weekends and evenings.

130

128. Eastern Parkway and Washington Avenue, 1900.

129. Central Park Automobile Permit #1.

130. Principal entrance to Prospect Park, Grand Army Plaza, 1906.

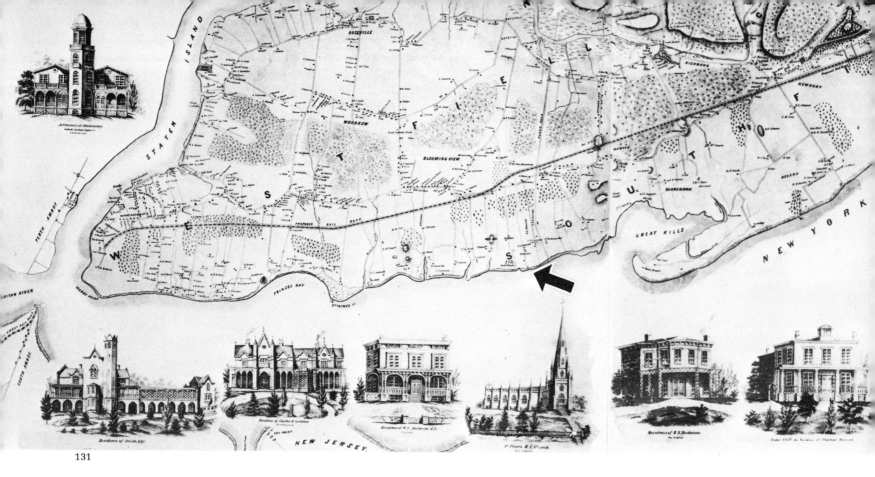

131

131. Map of Staten Island, 1853. Olmsted's farm is indicated by the arrow.

132. Olmsted's farmhouse, much altered but still in existence.

133. Pear trees still being sold from the farm by Olmsted's brother John. *Hagadorn's Staaten Islander,* 1856.

Olmsted operated a farm on Staten Island from 1848 to 1854, importing and propagating nursery stock for sale to farmers and landowners on the island: He sold also to landscape gardeners and no doubt assisted in choosing sites for trees and plantings. The view from his farmhouse across New York Bay he sometimes found "wondrous beautiful." Describing the places his view encompassed, he came uncannily close to enumerating the elements comprising the new federal park facility now being established: Gateway National Recreation Area.

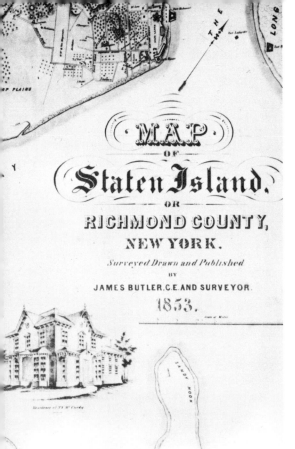

132

Post Office, will receive immediate attention.

mh15 3mpd

Pear Trees.

PEAR TREES of the best French varieties, upon quince roots, (coming into immediate bearing) and of good size. Trees delivered free upon this island. Mail address,

J. H. OLMSTEAD,

mh29 4w

Southside, S. I.

WARDLE'S SOLUBLE INDIGO.

THIS preparation meets all the objections hitherto made by the washerwoman, to the blue now warranted

133

134

135

134, 135. Staten Island views, 1880's.

136. Fourteen Recommendations made in Olmsted's Staten Island Improvement Commission Report.

A document extraordinary for its scope and completeness, the 1871 Staten Island Report dealt with a spectrum of interconnected environmental matters, from hygiene, especially with regard to malaria, to the matter of traffic networks. The primary intent was to solve its malaria problem and thus establish the island as a desirable residential area in the metropolis. Staten Island itself was most attractive, and Olmsted came back to live there while working on Prospect Park.

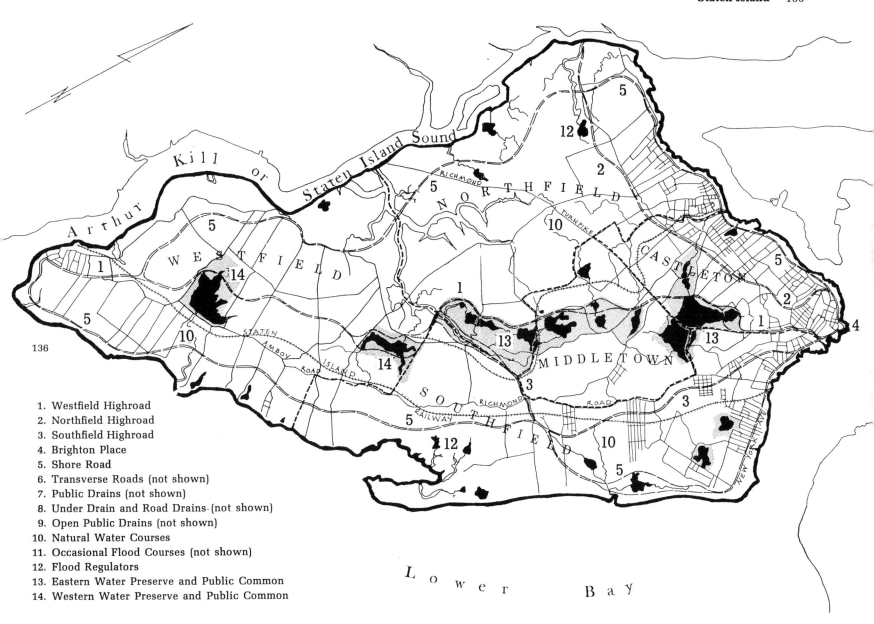

136

1. Westfield Highroad
2. Northfield Highroad
3. Southfield Highroad
4. Brighton Place
5. Shore Road
6. Transverse Roads (not shown)
7. Public Drains (not shown)
8. Under Drain and Road Drains (not shown)
9. Open Public Drains (not shown)
10. Natural Water Courses
11. Occasional Flood Courses (not shown)
12. Flood Regulators
13. Eastern Water Preserve and Public Common
14. Western Water Preserve and Public Common

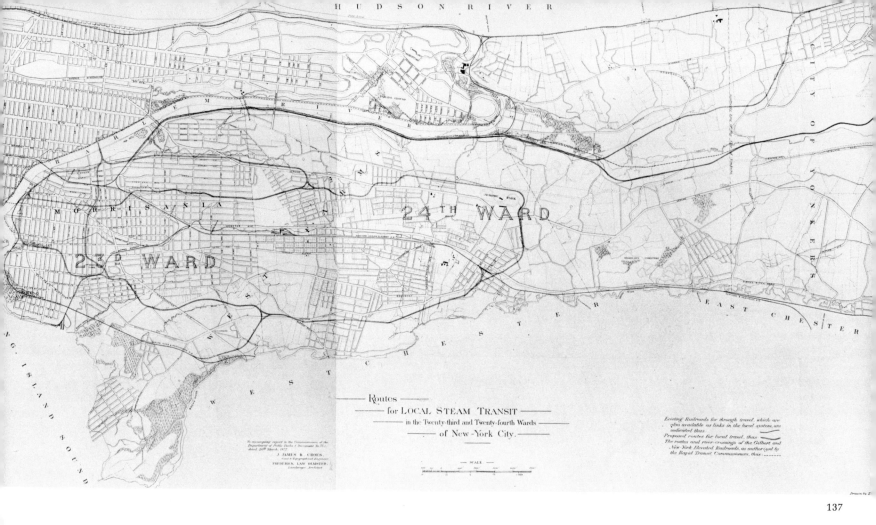

Routes
for LOCAL STEAM TRANSIT
in the Twenty-third and Twenty-fourth Wards
of New-York City.

137. The 23rd and 24th Ward (Bronx) local
   steam transit route plan, 1877.

138. View of the 23rd and 24th Wards looking
   south from High Bridge water tower, 1900.

Beyond his recommendations for development of the Bronx in accord with its own particular topography, Olmsted, together with civil and topographical engineer James Croes, devised a local steam transit rail system for the Bronx. Local, circuit, and through travel lines were carefully planned and were to come in advance of the final development of streets with their own traffic pattern, which were to be made integral. These, like other plans by Olmsted for New York, were not followed.

138

139. Sewer construction meets the New York Central Railroad tracks at the intersection of Broadway and 230th Street, Bronx, 1904.

140. Steam locomotive at the Fordham Road Station, Bronx, before 1900.

141. Construction of the Riverdale Avenue ramp opposite 232nd Street in the Bronx, 1928.

139

140

141

Heavy concrete retaining walls for straight roadway construction is avoided when streets follow topographical contours. In his Bronx reports Olmsted makes the point that "If a man . . . wishes to drive a horse of ordinary quality with a light wagon to another point 180 feet higher on a hillside, he can do so in shorter time upon a curved road 800 yards in length than up on a straight road of 600 yards." An automobile would, of course, require more fuel to overcome the grade.

Brief Report upon Rockaway Point.

I have examined the sea coast from
below Long Branch to beyond Far Rockaway
and found nowhere else natural advantages for a popular summer resort equal to those of the property
lately purchased by Mr. Attrill.

Its outer beach is in several respects
better than the beaches of Long Branch,
Seabright and Coney Island. It is in-
ferior in none. The water is clearer and the
surf more regular.

There is an admirable inner beach for still-water
bathing, a good harbor for the largest yachts,
quiet land-locked water for regattas, sailing,
fishing and shooting and a perfect driving
beach five miles in length swept
by the sea breeze, all which conditions are lacking at Long Branch and at
Manhattan and Brighton Beaches.

There is a site for a range of buildings
half a mile or more in length, close upon
the sea beach more elevated and less liable
to disturbance in storms than any corresponding
site at Coney Island or Long Branch. I believe

the sea breeze to be more stronger and steadier
and the mean summer temperature lower than
at either of these places.

There are no serious difficulties in the way
of drainage and sewerage and the sanitary conditions are decidedly superior to those of Coney Island.

I have found the Mr. Attrill's property
at disadvantage only in that it has none of
visitors. This I believe to be due to certain shallow
pools of fresh water upon it and a thick growth of
bushes about them. Both these objectionable
conditions may be perfectly remedied.

F.L.O.

N.Y. 16th Sep. 1874.

142

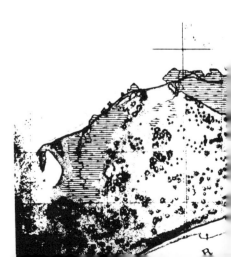

the sea breeze to be stronger and steadier
and the mean summer temperature lower than
at either of these places.

    There are no serious difficulties in the way
of drainage and sewerage and other sanitary conditions are decidedly superior to those of Coney Island.

    I have found Mr. Attrill's property
at disadvantage only in that it has more mus -
kitoes [sic]. This I believe to be due to certain shallow
pools of fresh water upon it and a thick growth of
bushes about them. Both these objectionable
conditions may be perfectly remedied.

NYC 16th Sept. 1879

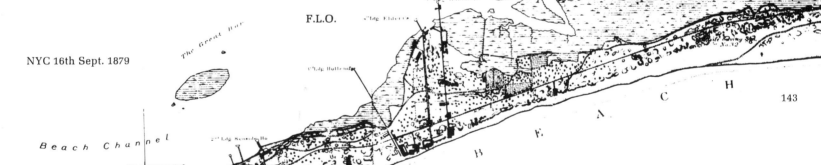

142. Brief Report upon Rockaway Point, 1879,
and transcription.

143. Map of Rockaway Beach, 1879.

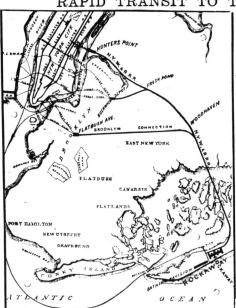

RAPID TRANSIT TO THE SEA.

Time, 30 Minutes to the Surf,

BY THE

N. Y., Woodhaven & Rockaway R.R.

A most beautiful ride across Jamaica Bay, on one of the longest Bridges in the World, to

ROCKAWAY BEACH

Hourly Excursions.

See Index on last page of Bullinger's Monitor Guide for time-table.

For **Fishing Excursions, Jamaica Bay** is without a rival within the limits of a day's trip from New York. Boatmen, with Boats to Hire for Hunting and Fishing purposes, are to be found at each Station.

The Beach is Nine Miles long, and is, throughout its length, one of the Finest on the Atlantic Coast, and Incomparably Superior to any other near New York, and affords **Surf and Still Water Bathing** and as Pleasant Promenading as can be asked for.

TICKETS for sale at the Depot of the New York, Woodhaven & Rockaway R.R., Hunter's Point; Long Island R.R., Bushwick and Flatbush Avenues, Brooklyn, and at Hunter's Point Annex, Pier 7 E.R.; James Slip, 7th St. and 34th St. Ferries, New York City.

Round Trip Excursion Tickets

FIFTY CENTS.

Liberal arrangements will be made for Large Excursion Parties by Societies, Lodges, Clubs, Schools, etc.

C. S. JUDSON, Gen'l Passenger and Ticket Agent, 68 Wall Street, New York.

144

144. "Rapid Transit to the Sea," 1883.

145. "Take the New York, Woodhaven and Rockaway Railroad to Rockaway Beach," 1880.

146. Bird's-eye view of Rockaway, 1880's.

145

146

In his formal report Olmsted elaborated on all conditions relative to the establishment of the resort that Mr. Atrill intended. Typically Olmstedian from psychology to fireworks to general advice, it was complete:

> Make the most that is practicable of these three elements—the great breadth of the oceanview, the surf tumbling at your feet and the expression of amplitude and liberality in your provision for general public entertainment...bring all your main structures into one line...to avoid flanking out the view of the sea.

147

How much of Olmsted's plan was followed is uncertain—the drawings
are lost—but it is known that he laid out the grounds and landscaped
the site for the world's largest hotel up to that time. It was 1,188 feet
long, 250 feet wide, and 40 persons could walk up its main stairway
arm in arm. Mr. Atrill went bankrupt and only one wing of the building opened, for about a month, to close down forever in 1881.

147. Rockaway Beach Hotel, 1881, the view printed on its letterhead.

148, 149. Rockaway Beach bathers, 1896.

148

149

150. Central Park South, 1968, photo by Peter Fink.

Nature and the city, the balance between them is man's to destroy, preserve, or mediate.

Frederick Law Olmsted was a practicing environmentalist a century before the word "ecology" came to have its current significance. He could look on a piece of land, understand the quality of its soil, ascertain the kinds of trees and grasses it could nourish, assay its capability to absorb and drain water, perceive the effect of prevailing winds and the action of the seasons. He knew the structure of the land and how it conducted the organic interchange of sun, air, water, and life. He also knew how to rearrange —not break or interfere with—these organic linkages in a viable, constructive way so that the land could serve man's purposes, because he was a firm believer in growth and progress.

In the same way he could also look at a city, understand the course of its development, predict the places where industry and trade would concentrate, where workers' houses would then follow, perceive where the problems of crowding would fester most, pinpoint the impending tangles of transportation and communication lines, foresee the inadequacies of provision for sewage and waste disposal with consequent pollution, and, when given the opportunity, could obviate these problems with remarkable vision.

In between these ecological and urban spheres, he knew how to mediate nature's way, providing for crowded cities great parks that re-created almost totally, for those deprived of it, the countryside, charming and complete, or providing in a country setting the amenities of towns.

It is ironic that just as the argument is being taken up all over the world as to whether man has actually succeeded in severing the links of the biosphere, the organic chain that binds his very existence on this planet, this country's, and perhaps the world's, most important environmental artist-engineer, Frederick Law Olmsted, comes to take his place on the stage of history.

Acknowledgments

The network of encouragement, support, and assistance that has made possible simultaneous exhibitions on Frederick Law Olmsted at the Whitney Museum of American Art in New York and the National Gallery of Art and the accompanying publications is simply too extensive to be described here. However, the basis for the Olmsted celebration and exhibition in New York was laid by Alice M. Kaplan and her fellow trustees of the J. M. Kaplan Fund, especially Joan K. Davidson and Raymond S. Rubinow. Further, as President of the American Federation of Arts, Mrs. Kaplan has provided the auspices for national circulation of the Olmsted traveling exhibition.

The Graham Foundation for Advanced Studies in the Fine Arts, of Chicago, has provided basic support that enabled the exhibition to come into existence.

Special thanks are due to Artemas P. Richardson, Joseph Hudak, and Mary Tynan of Olmsted Associates, Inc., Brookline, Massachusetts, for their patient and extensive cooperation. Both visual materials and research assistance have come in generous measure from Albert K. Baragwanath and Charlotte LaRue of the Museum of the City of New York; Gail K. Schneider of the Staten Island Institute of Arts and Sciences; Elizabeth Cromley of New York City; Vincent Seyfried of Garden City, New York; Dr. Theodore Kazimiroff of the Bronx, New York; Elizabeth White and Marie Spena of the Brooklyn Public Library; John H. Lindenbusch and James Hurley of the Long Island Historical Society; Dennis Loy of The New York Public Library; Donald Simon of the Department of Parks, Recreation and Cultural Affairs of New York City; Wilson Duprey of the New-York Historical Society; and the Berry-Hill Galleries of New York City.

Jean McClintock and Elliot Willensky of the Frederick Law Olmsted Association of New York have made generous contributions of time and effort to this celebration. Margaret Goldwater of the Olmsted Sesquicentennial Committee has devoted herself to the extensive factual and graphic research involved in the preparation of the publications and exhibitions.

Lastly, the noted Olmsted scholar Charles McLaughlin of Washington, D.C., has provided to many of those connected with Olmsted studies, including myself, not only graphic materials but also something that is most difficult to assess but which can be described as a kind of inspiration.

I am sincerely grateful to all the above.

WILLIAM ALEX

Sources of Illustrations

Note: *Central Park Reports* refer to the *Annual Reports of the Board of Commissioners of the Central Park. Brooklyn Parks Reports* refer to *Brooklyn Parks Department Annual Reports.*

Text

1. Museum of the City of New York. 2, 4. Eno Collection, Prints Division, New York Public Library. 5. Photo by I. Underhill. Brooklyn Picture Collection, Brooklyn Public Library. 6. Drawing by Frederick Law Olmsted in his *Journey Through Texas,* 1857. 7. Eno Collection, Prints Division, New York Public Library. 8. *Central Park Reports,* 1860. 9. Courtesy of Olmsted Associates, Inc., Brookline, Mass. 10. *Central Park Reports,* 1864. 11. Courtesy of The New-York Historical Society, New York City. 12. *Appleton's Journal Art Supplement,* 1869. 13. Courtesy of The Garden Library, Dumbarton Oaks, Washington, D.C. 14–17. *Central Park Reports,* 1872, 1862, 1868, 1862.

Illustrative Portfolio

1. Map Division, New York Public Library. 2. Courtesy of Olmsted Associates, Inc., Brookline, Mass. 3. V. Prevost, *Central Park in 1862.* Stuart Collection, New York Public Library. 4. I. N. Phelps Stokes Collection of American Historical Prints, Prints Division, New York Public Library. 5. V. Prevost, *Central Park in 1862.* Stuart Collection, New York Public Library. 6. Frederick Law Olmsted Papers, Manuscript Division, Library of Congress. 7. Courtesy of Olmsted Associates, Inc., Brookline, Mass. 8. Frederick Law Olmsted Papers, Manuscript Division, Library of Congress. 9–10. Museum of the City of New York. 11. Courtesy of The New-York Historical Society, New York City. 12. Courtesy of Olmsted Associates, Brookline, Mass. 13. Humphrey Repton, *Sketches and Hints on Landscape Gardening,* 1794. Courtesy of The Garden Library, Dumbarton Oaks, Washington, D.C. 14. Humphrey Repton, *Fragments on the Theory and Practice of Landscape Gardening,* 1816. Courtesy of The Garden Library, Dumbarton Oaks, Washington, D.C. 15–23. Museum of the City of New York. 24. *First Annual Report of the Board of Commissioners of the Department of Public Parks,* 1871. 25–27. *Central Park Reports,* 1860. 28. V. Prevost, *Central Park in 1862,* Stuart Collection, New York Public Library. 29. Photo by G. Rockwood. Picture Collection, Division of Local History and Genealogy, New York Public Library. 30. *Valentine's Manual,* 1862. Courtesy of The New-York Historical Society, New York City. 31. Courtesy of Olmsted Associates, Inc., Brookline, Mass. 32–36. *Central Park Reports* 1862, 1862, 1858, 1865, 1862. 37–40. Museum of the City of New York. 41. Courtesy of The New-York Historical Society, New York City. 42–47. Museum of the City of New York. 48. Photo by Ormsbee. Courtesy of Olmsted Associates, Inc., Brookline, Mass. 49–50. Eno Collection, Prints Division, New York Public Library. 51. *Third Annual Report,* Board of Commissioners of the Department of Public Parks, 1873. 52. Courtesy of Olmsted Associates, Inc., Brookline, Mass. 54–55. Museum of the City of New York. 57. Frederick Law Olmsted Papers, Manuscript Division, Library of Congress. 64–66. Photo by J. S. Johnston. Collections of the Library of Congress. 67. Museum of the City of New York. 68. Photo by E. Campbell. Collections of the Library of Congress. 69–70. Collections of the Library of Congress. 71–73. *Central Park Reports,* 1862, 1863, 1864. 74. Museum of the City of New York. 75. Courtesy of The New-York Historical Society, New York City. 76. Frederick Law Olmsted Papers, Manuscript Division, Library of Congress. 77. Museum of the City of New York. 78–79. Mabel Parsons Gift, Museum of the City of New York. 80. Courtesy of Olmsted Associates, Inc., Brookline, Mass. 81–82. Picture Collection, Division of Local History and Genealogy, New York Public Library. 83. Courtesy of The Garden Library, Dumbarton Oaks, Washington, D.C. 84. *West End Avenue,* issued by the West End Avenue Association, New York, May, 1888. 85. Courtesy of Berry-Hill Galleries, New York City. 86. Photo by G. Brainard. Brooklyn Picture Collection, Brooklyn Public Library. 87. Museum of the City of New York. 88. Picture Collection, Division of Local History and Genealogy, New York Public Library. 90. *Woman's League for the Protection of Riverside Park,* 1926. Division of Local History and Genealogy, New York Public Library. 91. Courtesy of Olmsted Associates, Inc., Brookline, Mass. 92. Frederick Law Olmsted Papers, Manuscript Division, Library of Congress. 93. Map Division, New York Public Library. 94. Courtesy of The Garden Library, Dumbarton Oaks, Washington, D.C. 95–96. Courtesy of the Long Island Historical Society. 97. *Brooklyn Parks Reports,* 1870. 98. Photo by Beal. Picture Collection, Division of Local History and Genealogy, New York Public Library. 99. *Brooklyn Parks Reports,* 1868. 101–102. Courtesy of Olmsted Associates, Inc., Brookline, Mass. 103. Photo by G. Brainard. Brooklyn Picture Collection, Brooklyn Public Library. 104–109. *Brooklyn Parks Reports,* 1885, 1885, 1885, 1872, 1869, 1872. 110–111. Brooklyn Picture Collection, Brooklyn Public Library. 112. *Brooklyn Parks Reports,* 1873. 113. Museum of the City of New York. 114–117. *Brooklyn Parks Reports,* 1887. 118. Photo by G. Brainard. Brooklyn Picture Collection, Brooklyn Public Library. 119. Courtesy of Olmsted Associates, Inc., Brookline, Mass. 120. *Brooklyn Parks Reports,* 1871. 121. Courtesy of the Long Island Historical Society. 122–123. *Brooklyn Parks Reports,* 1874. 124. Brooklyn Picture Collection, Brooklyn Public Library. 125. *East Parkway and Boulevards in the City of Brooklyn,* 1873. Courtesy of the Long Island Historical Society. 126. Frederick Law Olmsted, *Observations on the Progress of Improvements in Street Plans,* 1868. Title page. 127. *East Parkway and Boulevards in the City of Brooklyn,* 1873. Courtesy of the Long Island Historical Society. 128. Brooklyn Picture Collection, Brooklyn Public Library. 129. Museum of the City of New York. 130. Photo by I. Underhill. Brooklyn Picture Collection, Brooklyn Public Library. 131. Map Division, New York Public Library. 132. Photo by Elizabeth Barlow. 133–135. Courtesy of Staten Island Institute of Arts and Sciences. 136. Courtesy of Bradford Greene, Staten Island, New York. 137. Courtesy of The Garden Library, Dumbarton Oaks, Washington, D.C. 138–141. Courtesy of Dr. Theodore Kazimiroff, Bronx, New York. 142. Frederick Law Olmsted Papers, Manuscript Division, Library of Congress. 143–145. Courtesy of Vincent Seyfried, Garden City, New York. 146. Drawing by J. Bachmann. Courtesy of The New-York Historical Society, New York City. 147. Courtesy of Vincent Seyfried, Garden City, New York. 148–149. Photo by Percy Byron, 1896. Museum of the City of New York. 150. Photo by Peter Fink, New York.

Cover photo: Courtesy of Dr. Eugene Trachtman, CIRCLE-SCAN Company, Red Bank, New Jersey.

Chronology

Public Parks and elected President and Treasurer of the Board. Vaux appointed landscape architect. Later in the year Olmsted resigned and then was reappointed landscape architect, while Vaux, who had similarly resigned, was appointed consulting landscape architect.

Dissolved partnership with Vaux.

1873 Worked actively on Central Park.

Traveled through New England and Canada with the H. H. Richardsons. Visited Mount Royal, Montreal, for the first time.

Worked, with Vaux, on plan for Morningside Park, New York.

1874 Issued report on Capitol grounds and Lafayette Square area, Washington, D.C.

1875 Offered a proposal for new stairways and terraces west of the Capitol.

Prepared plan for Riverside Park and Avenue, New York.

1876 Presented the plan for the laying out of the 23rd and 24th Wards of New York, which was followed a year later by a report for local steam transit routes for the 23rd and 24th Wards (the Bronx).

Published, with Leopold Eidlitz and H. H. Richardson, a plan for the completion of the New York State Capitol Building at Albany, New York.

1878 Removed from his position as Superintendent of the Bureau of Design of the New York Department of Public Parks for political reasons.

Traveled through England and Europe.

Began actively campaigning for the preservation of Niagara Falls.

1879 Submitted plan for the development of Rockaway Point, New York.

Worked on Capitol grounds in Washington, D.C., and Boston parks. His involvement with Boston park system, which continued through 1893, resulted in Boston's "emerald necklace," a continuous system of parks and parkways.

1883 Bought house in Brookline, Massachusetts, which became his permanent home and professional headquarters.

Presented preliminary map for Belle Isle Park, Detroit.

Worked on plans for many private estates.

1884 Asked to help conduct first civil-service examination in landscape gardening given by New York Department of Public Parks.

1886 Published plan for Franklin Park, Boston.

1887 Revised general plan, with Vaux, for Morningside Park, New York.

General plan, with Vaux, for the improvement of Niagara Falls.

Visited Palo Alto, California, to begin plan for Stanford University.

1888 Began design of the Biltmore estate.

1891 Worked on plan for World's Columbian Exposition, Chicago.

Adviser on park system for Louisville.

1893 Worked with William Ware on a report on the occupation of a new site for Columbia University, New York City.

1894 Worked on plan for Cincinnati park system.

1895 Retired from professional practice.

1903 Died August 28.

Bibliography

General

Fabos, Julius G., Gordon T. Milde, and V. Michael Weinmayr. *Frederick Law Olmsted, Sr.: Founder of Landscape Architecture in America.* Amherst, Mass., 1968.

Fein, Albert, ed. *Landscape into Cityscape: Frederick Law Olmsted's Plans for a Greater New York City.* Ithaca, N.Y., 1967.

Huth, Hans. *Nature and the American: Three Centuries of Changing Attitudes.* Berkeley, Calif., 1957.

McLaughlin, Charles C., ed. "Selected Letters of Frederick Law Olmsted." Unpublished doctoral dissertation, Harvard University, 1959.

Marx, Leo. *The Machine in the Garden: Technology and the Pastoral Ideal in America.* New York, 1964.

Miller, Perry. *Nature's Nation.* Cambridge, Mass., 1967.

Mumford, Lewis. *The Brown Decades: A Study of the Arts in America, 1865–1895.* New York, 1931.

Nash, Roderick. *Wilderness and the American Mind.* New Haven, Conn., 1967.

Olmsted, Frederick Law, Jr., and Theodora Kimball, eds. *Frederick Law Olmsted, Landscape Architect, 1822–1903.* 2 vols. New York, 1922.

Olmsted Papers, Library of Congress.

Peterson, Jon Alvah. "The Origins of the Comprehensive City Planning Ideal in the United States." Unpublished doctoral dissertation, Harvard University, 1967.

Schlesinger, Arthur M. *The Rise of the City, 1878–1898.* New York, 1938.

Smith, Henry Nash. *Virgin Land: The American West as Symbol and Myth.* Cambridge, Mass., 1950.

Sutton, S. B., ed. *Civilizing American Cities: A Selection of Frederick Law Olmsted's Writings on City Landscapes.* Cambridge, Mass., 1971.

Tunnard, Christopher. *City of Man.* New York, 1953.

White, Morton, and Lucia White. *The Intellectual Versus the City.* Cambridge, Mass., 1962.

The Picturesque Tradition: Viewing Nature Through a Claude Glass

Chadwick, George F. *The Park and the Town: Public Landscape in the 19th and 20th Centuries.* New York, 1966.

Downing, Andrew Jackson. *Rural Essays.* New York, 1869.

————. *A Treatise on the Theory and Practice of Landscape Gardening.* New York, 1844.

Gilpin, William. *Forest Scenery.* 2 vols. London, 1791.

Hipple, Walter John, Jr. *The Beautiful, the Sublime and the Picturesque in Eighteenth Century British Aesthetic Theory.* Carbondale, Ill., 1957.

Hussey, Christopher. *The Picturesque.* London, 1927.

Loudon, John Claudius, ed. *The Landscape Gardening and Landscape Architecture of Humphry Repton, Esq.* London, 1840.

Olmsted, Frederick Law. *The Cotton Kingdom: A Traveller's Observations on Cotton and Slavery in the American Slave States.* New York, 1861. New ed., with introduction by Arthur M. Schlesinger. New York, 1953.

————. *A Journey in the Back Country.* New York, 1860.

————. *A Journey in the Seaboard Slave States, with Remarks on Their Economy.* New York, 1856.

_____. *A Journey Through Texas; or, a Saddle-Trip on the South-western Frontier: With a Statistical Appendix.* New York, 1857.

_____. *The Slave States Before the Civil War.* Harvey Wish, ed. New York, 1959.

Price, Uvedale. *On the Picturesque.* London, 1810.

Roper, Laura Wood. "Frederick Law Olmsted and the Western Texas Free-Soil Movement" *American Historical Review,* LVI (October, 1950): 58–64.

_____. "'Mr. Law' and *Putnam's Monthly Magazine:* A Note on a Phase in the Career of Frederick Law Olmsted." *American Literature,* XXVI, No. 1 (March, 1954): 88–93.

Central Park

Central Park Commissioners. *Annual Reports of the Board of Commissioners of the Central Park.* 1858–1870.

Olmsted, Frederick Law, Jr., and Theodora Kimball, eds. *Frederick Law Olmsted, Landscape Architect, 1822–1903.* Vol. II: "Central Park as a Work of Art and as a Great Municipal Enterprise." New York, 1922.

Reed, Henry Hope, and Sophia Duckworth. *Central Park: A History and a Guide.* New York, 1967.

Civil War Interlude

Maxwell, William Quentin. *Lincoln's Fifth Wheel.* New York, 1956.

Nevins, Allan, and Milton Halsey Thomas, eds. *The Diary of George Templeton Strong.* Vol. III: *The Civil War 1860–1865.* New York, 1952.

Olmsted, Frederick Law. *Hospital Transports: A Memoir.* Boston, 1863.

_____. "The Yosemite Valley and the Mariposa Big Trees: A Preliminary Report (1865) by Frederick Law Olmsted," Laura Wood Roper, ed. *Landscape Architecture,* XLIII, No. 1 (October, 1952): 13–25.

Royce, Josiah. *California from the Conquest in 1846 to the Second Vigilance Committee.* New York, 1948.

Wormeley, Katherine Prescott. *The Other Side of the War.* New York, 1889.

Prospect Park

Brooklyn Park Commissioners. *Brooklyn Parks Department Annual Reports, 1860–.*

Lancaster, Clay. *Prospect Park Handbook.* New York, 1967.

The New York That Might Have Been

Fein, ed., *Landscape into Cityscape, op. cit.,* pp. 173–300, 349–73, 375–82.

Sutton, ed., *Civilizing American Cities, op. cit.,* pp. 23–42, 52–99.

Small Parks

Brooklyn Park Commissioners. *Brooklyn Parks Department Annual Reports,* 1867, 1871.

Fein, ed., *Landscape into Cityscape, op. cit.,* pp. 333–41, 343–48, 441–57.

Index

Numerals in italic type are page numbers of illustration captions.